Nonprofit Organizations

NONPROFIT ORGANIZATIONS

Challenges and Collaboration

Alfred Vernis, Maria Iglesias, Beatriz Sanz

and

Àngel Saz-Carranza

PROPERTY OF

NOV 2 9 2006

THE FOUNDATION CTR

palgrave
macmillan

First published 2006 by
PALGRAVE MACMILLAN
Houndmills, Basingstoke, Hampshire RG21 6XS and
175 Fifth Avenue, New York, N.Y. 10010
Companies and representatives throughout the world

PALGRAVE MACMILLAN is the global academic imprint of the Palgrave
Macmillan division of St. Martin's Press, LLC and of Palgrave Macmillan Ltd.
Macmillan® is a registered trademark in the United States, United Kingdom
and other countries. Palgrave is a registered trademark in the European
Union and other countries.

ISBN-13: 978–1–4039–8635–1
ISBN-10: 1–4039–8635–5

This book is printed on paper suitable for recycling and made from fully
managed and sustained forest sources.

A catalogue record for this book is available from the British Library.

A catalog record for this book is available from the Library of Congress.

10   9   8   7   6   5   4   3   2   1
15   14   13   12   11   10   09   08   07   06

Printed and bound in China

CONTENTS

LIST OF FIGURES AND TABLES

Figures

Tables

CHAPTER I

Introduction

A Changing Environment that Affects Nonprofits

Surely, most people in nonprofit organizations[1] will readily recognize that their management practices have improved considerably in recent years. Several international studies from the 1990s emphasize the growth experienced by the third – or nonprofit – sector. Some of the most relevant examples include McCarthy, Hodgkinson and Sumaruwalla (1992), Salamon (1995), and Salamon and Anheier (1997). For instance, a comparative study undertaken by Johns Hopkins University (1997) reveals that, in the 1980s, one out of every seven new jobs in France belonged to the third sector, while in Germany the number was only slightly lower: one out of eight. Specifically, French nonprofits employed 578,106 people on a full-time basis and 431,181 part-time workers (Le Monde, February 3, 1998). The Organization for Economic Cooperation and Development (OECD) estimates that the number of Northern civil society organizations with international programs grew from 1600 in 1980 to more than 2500 in 1990. At the same time, within the developing world, the number of local civil society organizations with a relief and development focus has also increased. The Alliance for a Global community reports that there are more than 250,000 Southern nonprofits.[2]

Until recently, nonprofit management improvements were thought to relate mostly to human resources, communications, fund-raising, strategic planning and so on. However, experience has shown a neglect of several other aspects when it comes to strengthening third-sector organizational skills. These aspects, which we will analyze in depth in this book, are associated with the changes shaping society and markedly affecting nonprofits' operations and interactions with all other social actors.

It has been widely accepted that contemporary democratic societies are built around three sectors: public administrations, business corporations and nonprofit organizations. Like a three-legged stool, these three sectors have to work together to drive societies toward balance. In an ever-changing, fast-paced environment, third-sector organizations need to possess the required capabilities to face new challenges and to continue to contribute to improving the lives of people and communities. In other words, these organizations must be capable of truly leading and remodeling the complex world of social intervention.

At the very heart of the current, complex environment, characterized by dynamism and fast changes, we find that all three sectors are closely related, one way or another, because they exchange ideas, resources and responsibilities. Outside changes – affecting them all – vary in nature: economic, political, demographic, value-related and social, as shown in Figure 1.1 (De Vita and Fleming, 2001).

It would be extremely time consuming – and beside the point in this book – to review in detail the changes currently underway in twenty-first-century societies. However, it is worth mentioning briefly some of these changes affecting the third sector and putting a strain on nonprofit organizations.

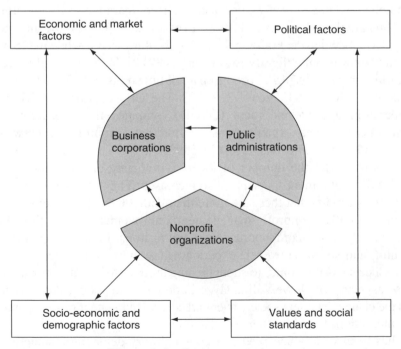

Figure 1.1   Environment changes

The Welfare State Reform

The so-called welfare state reform[3] has brought about very significant consequences for many non-governmental organizations (NGOs). What is commonly known as welfare pluralism (Taylor, 1992) is building a new arena for nonprofits to operate.

Evers and Svetlik (1993) uses what he calls the welfare triangle to gain an understanding of welfare pluralism (Figure 1.2) and the variety of actors primarily involved in building a welfare State in Western democratic societies. All the areas in the triangle may be best explained by means of an example: home assistance services for the elderly. First, relatives and neighbors are the key care providers for senior citizens; occasionally, these actors are viewed as the informal sector, and some authors even refer to this group as the fourth sector. Secondly, there is also an intermediate sector, composed of assistance and company providers and nonprofits in general. These organizations may provide these residential care services as subcontractors for public administrations or as direct suppliers to families and the elderly themselves. Thirdly, the market also includes business organizations offering their services to each group of actors. As a result of overall population ageing, most Western nations are experiencing a significant growth in the home-care service-providing industry. Finally, public administrations are indeed responsible for guaranteeing adequate services for their elderly constituencies. Therefore, Evers' welfare triangle shows the intermediary role awarded to nonprofits by welfare pluralism.[4]

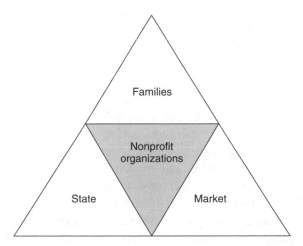

Figure 1.2 Welfare Triangle. *Source*: Evers and Wintersberger (1990)

In view of the actual (or imaginary) risk that the State neglects many of the social problems affecting society, letting the third sector deal with them, it is important for nonprofit organizations to rise to the challenge of explaining their role in this new welfare State – also called the relational state (Mendoza, 1995) – we are all building together. Volunteer associations are neither – and should not be – an obstacle for welfare State improvements nor allies of "privatization" or "anti-state" movements.

In short, public administrations are increasingly turning to nonprofit organizations to provide some of their services, and this is a source of tension for nonprofits. Surely, this tension would be appeased if this growing relationship between the third and public sectors was not viewed as exclusively abiding to market rules. Instead, new collaboration mechanisms should be devised for these cross-sector relationships.[5]

Competition ←——→ Collaboration

The Influence of Media and New Technologies

The changes brought about by the increasing significance of communications media constitute economic and market forces that also bear a relevant influence on nonprofit organizations. In the age of communications, some social organizations view the media as crucial for survival, using all available mechanisms and forms without restriction, even disregarding the sector's or organization's intrinsic values. Thus, some civil society organizations have decided to become involved in charity shows that undermine and blur the real work of most nonprofits. In the long run, these mass media interventions end up jeopardizing society's fragile trust in the third sector.[6]

Changes resulting from the new technologies gradually introduced in the third sector are also instrumental. These changes span from nonprofits' management improvements in areas such as internal and external communications, fund-raising, volunteer work and so on, to new venues in social advocacy and activism. The so-called *cyberactivism* has become very popular among nonprofits and social movements. New information technology breakthroughs have made demonstrations such as the ones carried out in Seattle (1999) and Genova (2001) possible.

Nonprofit organizations are challenged to adequately exploit the opportunities afforded by communications means and new technologies to improve their work and enable their workers – both volunteers and employees. However, they should not forget that the media often only seek to increase their ratings through high-impact, short-term, even tragic news. In addition, nonprofits must be the leading advocates for universal, top-quality Internet access. Hence, this new communications-based society is constantly straining nonprofits, which need to find a balance between the urge to communicate and the respect for their mission and values.

Enhancing Civil Involvement Through New Social Movements and Volunteer Work

A change gradually consolidating in many democratic countries is the increasing involvement of citizens in NGOs and social movements. Although domestic third sectors in Western nations have developed in different ways as a result of their political backgrounds (Cattacin, 1996) or social origins (Salamon and Anheier, 1998), their current boom and growth are evident. Beyond the sector's development and the special upsurge in volunteer work, individuals are becoming more and more aware of their need to be co-responsible for their own welfare and that of society as well. Voluntary civil involvement must take a share of responsibility for community issues. Trying to solve the severe problems caused by traffic, housing deficiencies, drug addiction, immigration, education, gender issues and so on, affecting most Western societies, just by increasing resources is bound to fail. Certainly, each citizen accounts for a share of the solution and the effort required.

This pragmatic vision should not be construed as applicable only to the United States, where political culture emphasizes individual responsibility and the State has long let private citizens handle severe social problems through volunteer organizations. Rather, it may be viewed as a public–private association, as is the case in several Northern European countries.

As Madrid (1997) puts it, historically, social citizenship has unfolded along two paths: mandatory and volunteer involvement. Nowadays, most public administrations seem to have fallen for the volunteer option. However, they should avoid two possible dangers: imposing too many regulations on volunteer work and trying to seize citizen involvement as their own. On the contrary, it should be the sector itself that regulates its own volunteer work. Volunteer civil involvement should be just that – civil and volunteer; no public administration should take any credit for mobilizing volunteers.

Precisely as a result of excessive public administration intervention, the incompetent charitable messages of some media and educational systems and a civic culture that fails to convey the significance of commitment, or – more often than not – as a consequence of a combination of causes we have yet to study in depth, nonprofit organizations are exposed to a new strain that derives from the fact that more and more individuals make one-time contributions instead of sustaining a continued commitment to them. Beck (2002) refers to the phenomenon of isolated involvement from a different, interesting viewpoint. He calls it "altruistic individualism" or "collaborating selfishness" and characterizes it as the attitude of many youngsters who contribute to third-sector organizations to "experience how individualism and social morals may be chosen again, while matching free will and individuality with living for others".

The organizations that have recognized these notions are learning to live with the ensuing tension: they work to mobilize as many people as possible for specific events, while they strive to elicit a long-term commitment from them.

| One-time involvement ◄───► Long-term involvement |

Increased Social Claim in Response to Inequalities, Injustices and Unsustainable Development

One of the most outstanding changes produced in nonprofit organizations is the increase in their social claim role. Citizens, gathered in consumer associations, environmental organizations, community associations and human rights organizations, raise a loud voice to protest against unfair situations often caused by international organizations and business companies, or by private or public interests.

However, this denouncing role also creates tensions inside nonprofits and between nonprofits and other social actors. NGOs should avoid any open confrontations with public administrations or companies to gain public exposure, or any situation that does not lead to specific solutions or proposals to solve problems. In these cases, social organizations will only succeed in making people see companies or administrations as part of the problem, when, in most cases, they are also part of the solution.

The World Social Forum: "Walking Slowly to Go Far"

Before, during and after the IV World Social Forum held in Mumbai, many voices rose to urge for no "more of the same" and to propose new paths to overcome dispersion and repetitive debates, seeking enhanced effectiveness for the alternative-world movement. After four successful editions, measured, in terms of their media impact and the number of attendants, it is clear now that the World Social Forum (FSM) has conquered its place in the world. It has managed to take the spotlight away from – no less – the Davos Economic Forum and has become an unavoidable reference not only for critics of the system, but also for government officials, businessmen and economists all over the world. Such a sudden success poses an imperative question: and now what? At the heart of the Forum, there is much debate as to immediate future paths, and the answers are far from unanimous. French farming leader José Bove believes "we have not yet been included among international decision-makers, along with states and economic powers." He insists "it is important for us to find the means to ensure our contributions are recognized even in institutional spheres – which may imply sitting at the table with the devil himself." Bernard Cassen, of ATTAC (France), goes even further, claiming the current Forum format should not be maintained, since it must influence "domestic, continental and international policies". He fears the movement risks "political impotence". Before the Forum, Italian leader Ricardo Petrella said that the movement "is not striving to build the strategic alliance required to accomplish some objectives", while he criticized the lack of "a common strategy". He believes we should "battle" against the credibility loss experienced by national parliaments and promote civil involvement at community and regional levels. Many others adhere to this position. Portuguese sociologist Boaventura de Sousa Santos also points out that there is a symmetrical conception of the hegemonic system when he states that "two globalizations are under way: one in civil society and another one in the neoliberal system. Some day, both will have to negotiate an agreement to promote a better and fairer world." (*Latin American Information Agency*, 02/13/2004, http://www.forumsocialmundial.org.br/)

Though sometimes neglected in the name of social co-responsibility, this role of NGOs should not be forgotten: it should be embraced determinedly. Otherwise, nonprofits may turn into mere service providers. Volunteers and their organizations have driven and should continue to promote a significant share of social denounce and transformation.

Social denounce unleashes a significant amount of tension for organizational management. Denouncing injustices caused by international organizations, public administrations, companies and so on may jeopardize their support – often economic in nature – to third-sector organizations.

This strain may be hard to deal with if organizations have but a few funding sources, since it may mean running out of funds to undertake their projects or services.[7]

Political action ◄──────► Service provision

A Greater Gap Between the Rich and the Poor in a Globalized World

Nonprofits operating in both developing countries and those devoting most of their efforts to assist the so-called Third World nations experience strong tensions on account of the seemingly scarce operating results. Year after year, several reports issued by international organizations describe the deepening differences between rich and poor countries. Also within nations, the gap between the privileged and the underprivileged is broadening as well. This may discourage people working at or supporting NGOs.

At the same time, the feeling that the deeply rooted causes of social disparities are not being addressed but only partially mitigated may also undermine support. This tension – so real and hard to offset – has several implications for social organizations. Those that are serious and have really understood the reason for their existence are working on several significant venues at the same time – all of them embodying a notion of development and solidarity far removed from short-term charity. Nonprofits that truly understand what it means to work in a globalized world operate, first, locally to secure a well-informed and committed social base. This approach may be explained by the fact that the structural causes underlying poverty require changes in the values and behavioral patterns of Northern hemisphere populations. Second, these organizations also work on a global level with international organisms and businesses to drive changes in economic and trade transactions between the North and the South.

Human Development Report

According to the 2003 Human Development Report published by the United Nations' Development Program, developing nations have made extraordinary improvements over the past thirty years. For instance, illiteracy rates have been reduced by half, up to 25%, and, in Southeast Asia, the number of people living on less than a dollar a day decreased by 50% in the 1990s. However, human development progress is painfully slow. As shown by the report, for many countries, the 1990s were marked by "despair". To cite a few examples, around 54 nations are poorer now than in 1990; in 21 countries, the number of people suffering from starvation has grown; there are more deaths among children under five years of age in 14 countries; elementary school enrollment rates are down in 12 countries, while in 34, life expectancy rates have also decreased. Another signal of the overall development crisis lies in the fact that the human development index (HDI, a measurement that factors in three human development dimensions: living a long and healthy life, getting an education and having a suitable living standard) has dropped as well. (http://hdr.undp.org)

It is important to stage projects for the Southern countries or in the areas surrounding major cities, but it is also paramount to rally in favor of sovereign debt abolishment or suitable housing conditions for the entire world.

Nonprofit organizations should avoid appealing to the charity of Northern populations through marketing techniques, since this approach does not lead to fostering their true commitment to remedying poverty and social injustice. This tension between charity and development surfaces in many managerial decisions made by third-sector officials and leaders. Again, organizations' missions and values become key factors.

Short-term charity ◄──────► Long-term development

An Increasingly Plural and Multi-cultural Society

In the previous section, we referred – with a necessarily simple-minded notion – to North and South as two well-differentiated parts in our globalized world. It is increasingly harder to tell where the North begins and the South ends. In any case, undeniably, the South will eventually become part of the North on account of the growing immigration waves. This unstoppable phenomenon also places significant strain on NGOs. A few of them are getting ready to work with unwilling émigrés who are forced to leave their countries to move to the Northern nations.

Only a few civil society organizations are currently working on conveying the values of solidarity and hospitality for immigrants to Northern peoples. Once again, surely, their most significant task hinges on raising awareness and education: teaching the Northern citizens to embrace cultural and religious plurality.

Indeed, most nonprofits work to support specific and noble causes –
such as education for Latin America, starvation remedies for Central
Africa, the struggle against AIDS in Africa, assistance for Down-
syndrome individuals, women's access to new technologies, educational improvements for urban teenagers through leisure-time programs
and so on. Nonprofits' success potential lies in their specificity – a
necessary feature that proves civil society's innovative capabilities.
Nevertheless, in a plural and multi-cultural society, excessive specificity – that is, an extremely "micro" and isolated focus – could lead to
social problems. Social organizations must attack specific causes while
embracing universal values.

| Particularism ◀——▶ Universality |

The Development of New Social Challenges

Underlying the tension we have just described, which stresses the need to
embrace more plural causes in an increasingly complex and specialized
world, there is another strain between the organizations that are still
operating in the same fashion and for the same causes they did twenty
years ago and those that are innovating and adjusting to society's new
challenges.

Still, the truth is that, as these developments unfold, new challenges
arise to confront committed civil society, demanding its attention.
These new social challenges include – to name a few – the growing
number of elderly people who live alone and have no relatives or
friends to provide them with care, the rising number of couples with
children who do not know how to share their parental responsibilities
after marital break-ups, the family and community problems resulting
from the fact that a significant share of youngsters have no access to
suitable housing and so on.

Nonprofit organizations should find new solutions for old social challenges
and new approaches to the new ones as well. Developing their capabilities for
constant innovation and ongoing learning is instrumental to reducing this
tension.

| Continuity ◀——▶ Innovation |

The Capacity Building Concept

In this new "relational society" setting, embedded in an evolving environment plagued by "tensions", the notion of capacity building – as we mentioned in our introduction to this chapter – becomes particularly relevant. Indeed, capacity building has turned into a recurring theme in institutional literature and a top priority in the agendas of public administrations, international institutions and nonprofit organizations. To prove it, the terms "capacity development", "institutional reform" and "good governance" abound in organizational policy and strategy documents, as well as in the objectives set for social action programs and projects. However, despite its increasing significance in institutional statements and practices, there is no single definition for capacity building.

At first, the notion was associated with the accomplishment of macroeconomic stability and economic growth in developing countries – especially at multilateral institutions such as the World Bank. Currently, the United Nations' Development Program (PNUD) states that capacity building refers to creating a society and supporting it to perform certain tasks and to achieve human development goals (set forth in the Millennium Statement).

Specifically, capacity building refers to the process of improving individual skills or strengthening the competencies of an organization or a group of organizations. McPhee and Bare (De Vita and Fleming, 2001) broaden this definition by means of two key concepts: the notion of mission – institutions should become stronger in order to pursue their missions better – and the notion of welfare – capacity building should ultimately serve to improve communities' living standards, a core aspiration for nonprofit organizations. This definition provides a suitable starting point.

For the purposes of this book, we intend to conceive capacity building as a process pursued by individuals, organizations and social systems to enhance their capabilities and performance in terms of their objectives, financial and human resources, and environment at large. This approach to the notion of capacity building implies the following:

- Capacity building requires direct engagement from the people and organizations involved.
- This process entails a time dimension that needs to be factored in: capacity building takes time.
- Capacity building involves many dimensions; hence, interventions will focus on several levels: individuals, organizations, sectors and institutions. Certainly, for a real impact, capacity building strategies must approach all levels simultaneously.

- Capacity building processes are meant to boost existing capabilities. Essentially, they focus on identifying leaders who are already active in communities or on reinforcing organizations that are already operational – rather than creating new ones.
- These processes seek to produce a true impact. Therefore, the effects of capacity building actions should be measurable, and these programs should incorporate measuring and validation systems based on several indicators that allow for ongoing follow-up of all stages.
- Environmental factors should be factored in as contingencies (both positive and negative) of capacity building possibilities and, also, as elements to be transformed.
- Capacity building requires great flexibility to adjust to local conditions. Additionally, there is no single approach to capacity building. All possible approaches resort to a set of strategies, notions, activities and resources focusing on mindset changes, technical capabilities development, and knowledge and skill transfers.

Indeed, this book is organized around the three levels we have identified in the capacity building notion (Figure 1.3). We believe it is necessary to work on all three at the same time in order to boost the third sector.

To begin with, it is necessary to work on the entire third sector on three directions simultaneously. First, collaboration ties should be built between nonprofit organizations and public administrations. These two sectors have interacted for years, but this relationship is often far from qualifying as a true collaboration. Secondly, it should also be convenient for nonprofits to approach private companies as well. Although exchanges with the private

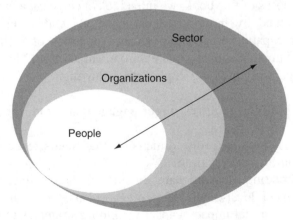

Figure 1.3   Capacity building levels

sector are less traditional, new and interesting collaboration venues are being explored.[8] Thirdly, nonprofits should also venture into relationships within their own sector. It is increasingly clear that sector consolidation hinges on greater collaboration among nonprofit organizations.

The first part of this book will deal with this level of capacity building, with a chapter devoted to each of the ties described above. Next, the book will focus on the organizational level in order to discuss two aspects we believe are crucial for third-sector strengthening: accountability and governance.

Society at large should hold nonprofit organizations accountable for all their operations – especially those individuals and institutions that provide their support. Nonprofits' accountability not only engulfs economic reporting and transparence, but it also entails project evaluation processes to measure mission accomplishment. At the same time, for accountability to be feasible, the third sector needs to have competent governance bodies, executive boards and trustees. In nonprofits, board members or trustees are accountable for organizations' accomplishments and failures – they are also in charge of setting strategic goals. If these bodies do not operate effectively, nonprofits may easily drift away from their missions. We shall devote a chapter to each of these topics.

Finally, we will explore the third level – that of individuals – and try to determine the specific competencies that people in different organizational strata should develop.

As nonprofit organizations rise to meet new challenges, they need to manage competent, committed and educated human resources. It is necessary to ensure ongoing competence enhancement for all third-sector members. Another chapter will be dedicated to this relevant issue.

Collaboration, Trust and Innovation Challenges Involved in the Development of Capacity Building Skills

Working on the three levels proposed in this chapter also implies facing the three most significant challenges for the third sector: collaboration, trust and innovation (Figure 1.4).

The Collaboration Challenge

In fact, to enhance their credibility, civil society organizations should collaborate with each other. Indeed, many people wonder why so many

Figure 1.4 Major challenges in each level

of them work in similar fields. Nonprofits will strengthen their positioning if they collaborate in joint projects. This cooperation should also stretch to engulf activities with public administrations and business companies. All organizations – public, private, for-profit or nonprofit alike – operating in a single territory may provide solutions for its specific conflicts. Relating to other nonprofits, public administrations and businesses embodies an ongoing challenge for most of the current third sector.

Conditions seem to have improved for this type of collaboration to blossom. In many public administration areas, public–private confrontational stances appear to have faded away. Now, the focus is on getting things done – if possible, with top quality. More and more companies are incorporating social responsibility to their modus operandi in an attempt to pay back to society for its opportunities. Most of the associative world has overcome the misguided charitable and patronizing models of the past and is presently working with its specific values, striving to accomplish true social improvements. Naturally, there is still a long way to go.

Unquestionably, in order to move toward this three-fold cross-sector collaboration, bilateral collaborations – between public administrations and nonprofits and between companies and nonprofits – should continue into the future. However, it is also necessary to build trust among all three sectors. Trust develops, partly, from interpersonal relationships. Public, private and nonprofit workers should reach out to their peers in other sectors, trying to understand their realities. The stereotypes coined by society – bureaucrats, yuppies and missionaries – should be left behind, for they prevent people from coming together.

Finally, it is necessary to understand that promoting three-fold collaborations may, in the long run, undermine and eliminate the boundaries between the three sectors. Soon enough, we will find we are networking.

The Trust Challenge

In spite of the expansion experienced by nonprofit organizations, as mentioned at the beginning of this chapter, some sectors still fail to understand their role in democratic societies. Nonprofits must prove to a significant share of the population that they are not merely charity institutions or service providers, but an essential pillar in today's societies. Although the trust inspired by this sector is generally higher than that of the public and private sectors, there has been a slight deterioration in recent years (Herzlinger, 1996).

Certainly, credibility may be enhanced through management improvements. Over the past few years, the third sector has made significant progress in human resources management, fund-raising, communications and financial management. As nonprofits mature, management improvements must decidedly focus on accountability, transparence and reporting to all supporters. If nonprofits learn how to explain their operations clearly, people who do not trust them now will come to realize that, in a market system, there are activities which cannot be undertaken by either business companies – for their lack of economic incentives – or public administrations – for their lack of organizational skills. This is the realm of civil society organizations.

Trust also stems from the reassurance that the trustees and members of nonprofits' boards do not seek these positions merely to build their reputations, but to serve as guardians of society's confidence in social organizations. Nonprofits should reinforce the roles of their trustees and board members so that they actually ensure the accomplishment of their organizations' missions.

The Challenge of Innovation

Nonprofits should innovate and experiment continuously. This is supposed to be one of the most outstanding features of the third sector. Sometimes, it seems that associations neglect this capability and customarily repeat past approaches, as if they had lost their innovating skills. They need to take risks to rise to increasingly harder challenges in their attempt to solve the new issues arising in democratic societies. Yet, it is also true that some organizations are already moving in this direction.

Capability development and continuous training for nonprofits' human resources also stand out as significant requirements for innovation. Organizations will be able to innovate if they rely on highly trained professionals. Third-sector leaders must strive to improve their professional skills. To enhance their operating performance, associations need managers and workers who are trained on new information technologies, project development techniques, financial and service management and so on. Ongoing education should become a regular feature in nonprofits' agendas.

Nonprofits: The Need to Go Beyond Effectiveness and Efficiency

Starting a nonprofit organization without having thoroughly developed its mission and a set of values to guide its operations is depriving it of its heart. Values – the differentiating factor in nonprofit organizations – must guide all the actions undertaken by civil society organizations (Figure 1.5). If these values are not clear and shared by all members and collaborators, or have not even been set forth, organizations may easily fall prey to external and internal contradictions. At the same time, organizations need to know their mission – the purpose of their existence – before they start operating in society.

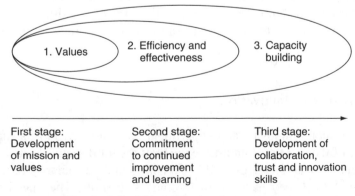

Figure 1.5   Nonprofit development stages

Nonprofits as Labs for Democratic Involvement

A glimpse at the values advocated by most nonprofit organizations would reveal the following: tolerance, freedom, justice, commitment, equality, responsibility, humanitarianism, citizenship, friendship, involvement, peace, non-violence, solidarity, respect for multiple cultures, environmental care and improved living conditions. Naturally, these values are not embraced by the third sector only; rather, this list constitutes a sample of the essential values of all democratic societies. However, these values and their enforcement should be especially reflected by civil society organizations and their leaders. When associations embody these values, they optimize their chances to becoming, first, true "democracy labs" for their members, and, second, open forums for people to explore new ideas. These organizations allow society not only to enhance the use of its resources, but also to open up to new voices and new projects — different to the public projects managed and even imposed by political and media powers. Indeed, by advocating these values, nonprofits perform a specific and unique task for society: they contribute to its governance.

For us, this is the first stage in building and developing well-managed nonprofit organizations. Hence, in our management model, organizational values hold a central position.

In 1998, we considered that "We should not fool ourselves: management and nonprofits have not gotten along very well until recently. So far, nonprofits have been managed with a lot of goodwill and very little reason. All too often, management has been perceived as opposed to the core values of third-sector organizations" (Vernis *et al.*, 1998, p. 15). We believe nonprofits have come a long way in management improvements over the past few years. Like other researchers in this field, we insisted then — and still do — that "society needs organizations that do good and do it well".

This is, in our opinion, the second stage in nonprofits' management improvements — the stage that should focus on improving organizational effectiveness and efficiency.

Yet, we believe that the impact of nonprofit organizations on the living conditions of needy people (in developed and in developing countries), on environmental protection, on community rights and opportunities and so on is still below our aspirations. We also believe nonprofits should enhance their capabilities to boost their results. This accounts for the third stage — surely the most important one — in nonprofits' management improvements. We have defined it as the capacity building stage.

All nonprofit organizations are heading toward the challenge of finding what developmental stage they are in. In that exercise, their chances for definite social legitimacy is at stake. Yet, let us not fool ourselves: social legitimacy does not come easy for mature nonprofits. The trust, collaboration and innovation challenges are hard to overcome. Additionally, nonprofits are weighed down by heavy burdens, which were probably great successes in their past records. Not long ago, religious institutions fostered a charity-oriented culture to help the poor and thus earn eternal salvation. The following leaders started out on a clean slate and created the paternalistic State in the belief that the State would fix all wrongs. And our present-day leaders are advertising the notion that economic development will manage to reach everyone: if the rich are indeed richer, the poor will be less poor. The picture becomes even more colorful when we add the media, which, for the most part, create their own charity shows with the purpose of raising their ratings. Among religious institutions, public administrations, business companies and mass media, nonprofit organizations have their own place. In addition, all sectors jointly conform to a common forum. Nonprofits' own sphere and, more importantly, the common forum built by all sectors must be consolidated over the next years – which will require stronger nonprofit organizations. This book intends to contribute its share to third-sector capacity building.

PART I

Collaboration

Nowadays, we group organizations operating in society in three sectors: businesses, public administrations and nonprofit organizations. Still, when we plot the three sectors on a chart, the boundaries among sectors are drawn to overlap, since these boundaries are increasingly blurred. Otherwise, on the following chart, where would we place, for instance, a nonprofit school receiving 90 percent of its operating funds from public agencies? Or a public company collecting 50 percent of its revenues from services and products sold in the market? Certainly, it is becoming increasingly hard to determine clear boundaries among the three sectors – between public, private and nonprofit ventures.

There is yet another reason to plot the three sectors as overlapping. Increasingly often, collaborations are built between nonprofits and public administrations (Section 1), between nonprofits and business corporations (Section 2) and between nonprofits themselves (Section 3) (Figure PI.1).[1]

In a relational society, the relationships between nonprofits, public administrations and businesses fall in the co-responsibility realm. Co-responsibility implies common objectives, specific responsibilities for each party to achieve these goals and the effective orchestration of this collaboration.

As collaborations grow and spread, the third sector needs to consolidate its role as a key link between citizens and all other sectors. "The quality of the services provided by third-sector organizations will help legitimize [...] the democratic system. Thus, all actors – administrations, corporations and nonprofits – will be forced to develop a relational, cooperative culture based on joint goal setting, responsibility allocation and the search for common consent, without jeopardizing their individual identities" (Castiñeira and Vidal, 2003).

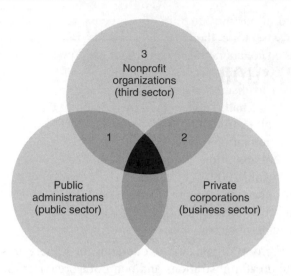

Figure PI.I   Sectors' overlappings. (*Source:* Elaborated by the authors)

Thus, the increase in collaborations is not fortuitous, since the past antagonism between sectors has decreased as actors have learnt to accept and be accepted by the others. In fact, the ongoing changes affecting today's world render collaboration an indispensable strategy – though not necessarily void of potential hazards or risks. Technological breakthroughs, both global and local interactions among actors and sectors, and the changes in public administrations' power and roles the 1980s have altered the nature and format of collaborations. Present society features have taken the notion of social corporate responsibility to the business community and drawn sectors closer to each other. Specifically, these features have been bred by knowledge and its effects on relationships, innovation and its ensuing dynamism, multiple cultures, risks – both for citizens and companies' reputations – and social inequalities and complexities, which have blurred the boundaries between sectors and actors, as well as society's interdependencies (Miralles, 2002). In any case, we are still in the initial approaches to understanding and gearing these collaborations – particularly, cross-sector collaborations, that is, those involving actors from the public, private nonprofit and private profit sectors. There is the danger that not all sectors move forward at the same speed and rhythm. In view of the interactions among actors, fruitful opportunities may be lost, and – worse yet – social maladjustments may occur. The next chapters intend to contribute the necessary elements for third-sector organizations to meet and overcome the challenges of future collaborations.

As we stated in our introduction, third-sector institutional strengthening depends on cross-sector collaborations – thus, the following three chapters in this book focus on collaborations. Focusing on nonprofits and their perspective, we will review collaborations between nonprofits and businesses first; then, we will proceed to discuss collaborations between nonprofits and public administrations to, finally, concentrate on collaborations among nonprofits themselves. Chapter structures and approaches differ slightly, varying in emphasis and connotations. However, one concept stands out in all three chapters: the collaboration continuum (Kramer, 1981; Taylor, 1990; Wolch, 1990; Austin, 2000). Throughout this book, collaboration is viewed as a continuum growing in intensity. In other words, collaboration is not made up by a set of clearly defined stages, allowing us to determine the specific phase undergone by a collaboration at any given point in time.

CHAPTER 2

Collaborations Between Businesses and Nonprofits: Approaching Corporate Citizenship

Sustainable Development as the Purpose of Collaborations

As mentioned in the introduction, social organizations face a significant challenge that entails looking beyond the individual advantages to be reaped by collaborations in an attempt to promote sustainable development through contacts with business companies. Both sectors are increasingly aware of the mutual dependence tying them both. Just as companies need nonprofits to approach the civil society, the third sector should not neglect the opportunity to design sustainable development in collaboration with companies.

Another strategic driver for nonprofits, closely related to the notion of sustainable development, is *society's self-regulation*. At a time when, in general, the State cannot reach society's multiple dimensions, the need to regulate them does not vanish. In view of that void, cross-sector collaborations may help structure and regulate society. Also, the *efficient utilization of available resources* constitutes a strategic driver for nonprofit organizations. Collaborations may provide synergies and coordination opportunities that enhance the exploitation of society's limited – often scarce – resources.

Sectors Come Together

In July 2001, the European Commission launched its *Green Book: Promoting a European Framework for Corporate Social Responsibility (CSR)*. The European Commission defines CSR as "companies' voluntary incorporation of social and environmental concerns to their trading operations and their relationships with their stakeholders" (European Commission, 2001).

Together for Africa

Under the motto "Together for Africa", Spain's Médecins Sans Frontières (MSF), Intermón Oxfam and the Spanish Red Cross, along with the transportation company MRW and Coca-Cola, launched, in late 2001, a campaign to collect the Spanish pesetas and other coins that would be lost during the national currency conversion to euros to provide assistance to African populations. Coin collection boxes were distributed by Coca-Cola and picked up by MRW.

One of the salient aspects of the campaign that came to an end in June 2002 was, certainly, its huge success in reaching the entire Spanish population. Collection boxes were everywhere; people knew about the campaign, and a total of around two hundred million coins of all kinds and denominations were collected throughout the campaign, amounting to over one billion pesetas ($7 million). Total revenues were somewhat below expectations, but there were no precedents to benchmark potential results.

It should be noted that society has especially valued the collaboration built among institutions, partners and media, and the fact that joint work has strengthened the ties between the three participating NGOs. Additionally, these contacts have been useful to ensure that large commercial areas open up to fair trade products and that these companies engage in future projects of this kind.

A year before, the OECD had reviewed its conduct manual for multinational companies. That same year, Kofi Annan, United Nations' Secretary General, proposed a world covenant to "match the creative forces of private business spirit with the needs of the disadvantaged and future generations" (Annan, 2000). On the one hand, the attitude toward the business sector is changing: companies are increasingly viewed as a necessary partner in improving society. At the same time, the expectations regarding the businesses' commitment to social development are growing as well. On the other hand, the overall attitude toward the nonprofit sector has also changed, and its relevance for society's well-being has been finally acknowledged.

The changes produced in power distribution constitute another key factor in driving cross-sector collaborations between businesses and social organizations. Nonprofits have approached businesses to try to rule "globalization". They have realized that sustainable development would be hard to accomplish without the business sector. The severe complexity of most social problems has forced the third and public sectors to engage the business community in the search for feasible solutions. Companies, in turn, have resorted to collaborations with third-sector organizations to respond to social demands, as well as to seize specific opportunities, which we will discuss later. Modern business theories recognize the significance of public image and social responsibility for companies and seem to draw away from the neoclassic business theory in this regard. Thus, modern principles try to harmonize corporations' self-satisfying imperative and an adequate relationship between business and society.

Collaborations between businesses and nonprofits evolve toward more proactive social actions. In other words, ever more frequently, firms undertake these collaborations of their own accord and as an end in itself, and not so much as a result of the need to "respond to society's demands". The evolution toward more proactive social actions conforms to the change businesses are experiencing in their connection to society. Corporate citizenship is a clearly proactive notion that, as pointed out by Lozano, acknowledges that business decisions encompass a range of dimensions – including the ethical dimension. Lozano (2001) emphasizes that the idea is not for companies to assume the role of the State or political action. Rather, they are expected to explore the civil dimensions of their operations. In addition, the confusion between public issues and State should also be avoided, leaving behind the notion that only the State bears a social responsibility (Lozano, 2001). Similarly, advocating a greater social corporate responsibility does not imply that laws are unnecessary; rather, it expects voluntary actions to go beyond current rules – possibly, even, setting the groundwork for future legislation (Miralles, 2002).

In a similar fashion, nonprofits move on to more proactive relationships with businesses instead of responding to individual situations. In fact, there has been a huge increase in the number of nonprofits that have devised codes of conduct to improve their management of relationships with companies. Thus, it is quite clear that both sectors are foregoing the reactive relational model of the past to embrace a more proactive mutual approach.

Another factor that shapes cross-sector relationships lies in the attitude to the other party involved. The two extremes found in relationships are confrontation and collaboration. Nonprofits will have to determine the type of relationship to be built according to its ideological-philosophical position along the ideological continuum, which spans from a pragmatic end to a purist extreme (Figure 2.1).

Certainly, nonprofits' positioning in this continuum is closely related to the renounce–denounce dilemma we have already discussed. Although at

Figure 2.1   The ideological continuum. (*Source*: Elaborated by the authors)

times "purist" positions may be necessary, for example in a denounce campaign that implies a confrontation, nonprofits are increasingly tending toward cross-sector collaborations.

Thus, both sectors, business companies and nonprofit organizations, seem to be experiencing a change in their mutual relationships, going from reactive and confrontational liaisons to proactive and collaborative relations (Figure 2.2).

Although, at present, both sectors need each other to accomplish their respective missions, experience shows that companies' contributions to the third sector are still rather modest. It has been estimated in several Western nations that only 10 percent of private contributions to nonprofits come from companies (Useem, 1987; Sciullo, 1993). Indeed, cross-sector collaboration is still rather new and immature. To prove it, no quantitative data on social activities are included in the annual reports of most large corporations (Ruyra de Andrade and Sotelo-Zuloaga Galdiz, 1999). Probably, this behavior derives from the fear that the amount invested in collaborations is unsuitable – either too high or low – and the uncertain reaction of shareholders to these collaborations. The multiplying perspective of collaborations between nonprofit organizations and business companies is significantly enhanced by the number of intermediary groups devoted to studying and boosting cross-sector interactions. These groups intend to promote this kind of activities from several standpoints. There are multilateral

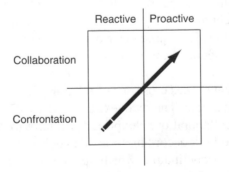

Figure 2.2   Matrix for relationships between companies and nonprofits. (*Source*: Elaborated by the authors)

programs, such as the World Bank's Business Partners for Development (www.bpdweb.org), special forums, such as the Caux Round Table (www.cauxroundtable.org), and corporate alliances or associations, such as the Prince of Wales International Leaders Business Forum (www.pwblf.org). Also, numerous research and education teams analyze this topic, such as the Center for Action Research on Professional Practice at the University of Bath (www.bath.ac.uk), the Boston College's Center for Corporate Citizenship of Boston College (www.bc.edu), the Social Enterprise Knowledge Center of Harvard Business School (www.hbs.edu), and the *Instituto Persona, Empresa y Sociedad* of Esade Business School (www.esade.edu).

Why do Nonprofits Collaborate?

The relationship models applied to the third and business sectors are numerous. Collaboration entails, unquestionably, one of the most complex forms. Unilateral donations, confrontations through awareness and denounce campaigns and periodical dialog are far less complex relational formats.

Nonprofits will choose their relationship mode – sporadic or confrontational – according to their philosophy, missions and present situation. Collaboration is, then, an option, though it is not always the most appropriate or advisable course to take. Each organization needs to determine whether collaboration is the most suitable format in view of its desired results. All in all, cross-sector collaborations between nonprofit and business organizations are growing in number.

Certainly, this growth has been brought about by the increasing outsourcing of several services traditionally provided by the State in the past, which has effectively expanded nonprofits' operating fields and, at the same time, has introduced companies to areas that used to be exclusively served by nonprofits. Thus, social organizations must compete with companies for resources. Oddly enough, both the social and business sectors have been forced to seek different kinds of mutual alliances to respond to this new scenario.

In any case, as we mentioned at the beginning of this chapter, collaborations should be essentially and ultimately pursued to accomplish sustainable development and to ensure a fairer and more compassionate society. Within that framework, let us find specific and operating drivers for collaboration, such as the ones we enumerate next.

Resources

The primary benefit for nonprofits that comes to mind when talking about cross-sector collaborations is financial. Although it is not necessarily the foremost driver in collaborations, an excessive dependence on public or foundation-based funding forces some nonprofits to seek other financing sources.

Another factor driving third-sector organizations to look for corporate support lies in the need to diversify funding. Public administrations tend to respond to changing agendas, which renders them unstable as funding sources. Contributions from private businesses do not usually entail this inconvenience.

Finally, many public administrations are reluctant to cover overhead. On the contrary, companies abide to less rigid standards when it comes to donations. Corporate funding tends to be more flexible and easier to implement.

Exposure and communications

Through collaborating companies, social organizations may find new communication channels to reach social sectors that eluded them in the past. This is highly valuable for the third sector either to ensure social support for their causes or to convey their advocacy message.

An additional benefit derived from cross-sector collaboration involves exposure. By means of collaborations with businesses, civil society organizations may enhance their visibility in business circles. Increased exposure opens new paths to prospective new partners. In this light, collaboration becomes a powerful tool for networking with other actors that may have an impact on nonprofits' operating areas. Also, once a collaboration has been built, others may follow in a highly beneficial chain effect.

Knowledge and new intervention areas

The ever-changing environmental conditions and new challenges faced by third-sector organizations turn companies into a significant source of knowledge and new methodologies that may add a great deal of value if applied to the nonprofit sector. Techniques to enhance efficiency and effective or entrepreneurial behaviors account for potential benefits for social organizations. At the same time, collaborations with business companies may introduce nonprofits to new operating fields.

Influential capabilities

Collaboration between nonprofits and business corporations generally implies an exchange not only in the technical terms associated with knowledge and intervention methodologies, but also regarding values and principles. Thus, collaborations allow for a mutual flow of influence on different perspectives that enrich both parties involved.

Why do Businesses Collaborate?

Like the social sector, the business sector has its own strategic and operating drivers to engage in collaborations. The strategic motivation that urges a company to collaborate with civil society is corporate citizenship. The search for a role that goes beyond economic benefits may become a strong determinant for business organizations to collaborate, on strategic grounds, with nonprofits.

Corporate Social Responsibility as a Collaboration Driver

Companies may collaborate with civil society organizations and engage in social activities out of a strong sense of corporate social responsibility, since collaborations embody one of the most visible mechanisms for this responsibility. According to Oster (1995), there are two major drivers for companies to selflessly develop social activities. The first stems from the notion of *returning a share of profits to society* – this notion recognizes that society has contributed to companies' profitability. The second one, instead, relates to the desire to *donate a share of corporation profits* – which does not entail an acknowledgement of society's contribution, but a strictly generous offering to society. Social actions are usually enabled by the first driver, whereas individual donations generally originate in the second one (Oster, 1995). Clearly, the notion of *returning a share of profits to society* constitutes a strategic concept and implies a greater awareness of corporations' role in society, as well as a stronger, more proactive commitment to social issues.

Operating Drivers Underlying Collaborations

The drivers propelling companies to collaborate with third-sector organizations in social actions differ in nature. For the sake of simplicity, we have classified them into several categories, though, actually, business companies collaborate with nonprofits for a myriad of reasons.

Marketing

Until the 1980s, consumers used to identify brands with various values but, oddly enough, the opposite phenomenon is presently taking over: brands place those values in consumers. Marketing drivers for cross-sector collaborations between business companies and nonprofits may be grouped into three large categories: institutional marketing, product marketing and market expansion (Austin, 2001a).

Businesses may undertake collaborations to embark on *institutional marketing* or to enhance their public relations – that is, to strengthen their image. Public image improvements imply a positive shift in companies' relations with critical social sectors, whose power to impair their brands is substantial. On the other hand, collaborations with nonprofits build bridges between civil society and companies. The business sector exploits not only social organizations' images but also their proximity to civil society. For companies, engaging a third-sector agent to improve society provides additional legitimacy, which in turn ensures greater future leverage and support from civil society. These relationships may be construed as a communication platform created by companies to bond with their communities and keep continuous ties with society.

Institutional marketing should also be regarded as an improvement in companies' public relations. The purpose of collaborations may be to prevent governmental intervention or to improve environmental conditions – relations with stakeholders that indirectly affect companies' business, such as nonprofits themselves and specific civil society segments. In short, companies try to better their surroundings, for a hostile environment definitely plays against any business.

Instead, collaborations intended to develop *product marketing* focus primarily on creating value for the product involved. Third-sector organizations, in this case, act as credentials and vouch for companies' social commitment. This is, clearly, the most common driver moving companies toward collaborations, although it is gradually losing momentum nowadays. Product marketing certainly implies a short-term approach by companies, whereas institutional marketing efforts are more long-term oriented.

Companies may also engage in collaborations with civil society agents to serve their *market expansion* strategies, reaching untapped population segments that used to be unknown to them. These sectors may be approached through the knowledge and image of social organizations. Collaborations enable companies to promote their products or brands among potential consumers who would otherwise be out of their reach. By joining a third-sector organization, companies manage to appeal to new, demanding, educated, critical and more socially committed consumers.

Human resources
Companies may be interested in collaborating with social organizations for reasons associated with their human resources. Collaborations driven by human resource purposes focus on employee development. In this process, businesses' human resources is actively empowered in several ways.

An initial positive outcome drawn by corporate human resources from social action lies in employee motivation, as a result of a sense of usefulness that grows in people. According to psychiatrist Rojas Marcos, this sense of purpose reduces psychological distress (Rojas Marcos, 2001). In addition, employees feel a renewed loyalty to their company. In fact, companies that contribute to civil society enjoy three times as much employee motivation as other companies (Useem, 1987), which leads to long-term performance improvements. Also, as employees come to value their company's social commitment, companies enhance their potential to retain highly qualified individuals.

Occasionally, collaborations are intended to *train* company employees. As companies and their personnel face new challenges, collaborations with nonprofits are often sought to develop new employee skills. The different environments in which employees find themselves when they participate in collaborations allow for the application of new methodologies and approaches, as well as for the development of special abilities to work in diversified teams. Also to be noted is the profound knowledge civil organizations have of their own sectors. Companies are trying to enter into fields that used to be the realm of social organizations.

Indeed, collaborating with nonprofits may account for a gateway to valuable technical and methodological knowledge.

Operating efficiency
Companies have also found a source of operating opportunities in social organizations. Purchasing goods and services from nonprofits may, often enough, enhance companies' effectiveness. Operating collaborations have grown on account of two significant changes:

1. Businesses have moved toward social sectors that used to be unknown to them. Hence, buying services from nonprofits becomes a highly sensible option.

2. In turn, social organizations have moved in the opposite direction: by competing with traditional suppliers from the business sector, nonprofits have increasingly offered their services to profit-oriented organizations.

Companies decide to buy goods and services from nonprofits for three different reasons (Vernis, 1998b):

1. First, private firms may purchase products or services from nonprofits simply because their offerings are the most competitive ones in the market.
2. Second, nonprofits' offerings may be good, though not the best in the market. In this case, companies purchase their services or products on account of the affinity between both organizations.
3. Finally, purchases may be the result of companies' intention to support specific social organizations.

In fact, although many an operating collaboration stems from this last option, many nonprofits ultimately become competitive providers.

Factors Determining Business Involvement and Partners Preferred by Businesses

The way in which companies stage their social activities is closely related to whether their motivation is strategic or operative, which in turn depends on their size. Larger companies start off by having a professional department specially devoted to this kind of activities, and the most committed ones go as far as including their involvement in social development in their mission statements. Instead, smaller companies do not usually pursue a planned social strategy and tend to act *ad hoc* (Useem, 1987). Some key factors influencing companies' decision to collaborate with nonprofits include the following (Useem, 1987; Smith, 1989; Oster, 1995):

*   *The size of their advertising and image-related expenses* is often associated with their interest in social action – mainly because of their exposure to the general public. The more companies are in contact with the public, the more inclined they are to become socially active.
*   Companies in *monopolistic markets* tend to become more involved in social improvements, possibly because of their larger benefits and their

greater need for public legitimacy resulting from their monopolistic nature itself.

- A highly significant factor lies in companies' *approach to their own interests*. Long-term-oriented companies usually include social welfare in their own set of interests. Similarly, companies that take into account their various stakeholders tend to be more willing to collaborate with the third sector. On the contrary, companies focusing on short-term operations and shareholders' interests are usually more reluctant to collaborate with social organizations. There is another factor, closely related to this notion, that significantly influences corporate attitudes toward collaborations with nonprofits: organizational culture. Companies whose organizational culture has traditionally emphasized social involvement are more prone to collaborating with nonprofits than those with an organizational culture that shows a lesser regard for social commitment.
- In a similar fashion, *the culture of the entire business sector* and geographical location are also influential factors in this process. Some industries are more collaboration-prone, whereas others seem more unwilling to collaborate. Additionally, in some locations companies are more used to social commitment than in other regions.

In any case, some of the factors affecting collaborations are not associated with companies or their environments. Third-sector organizations constitute one of these factors. A thoroughly well-organized third sector – especially keen on communications and fund-raising – enhances the chances for business involvement in social issues. Another relevant factor lies in the domestic tax policies, since deductible social investments account for a significant appeal for businesses. Another factor is State involvement. Oddly enough, a lesser State involvement in social services is usually a deterrent for business social commitment (Useem, 1987). Finally, cross-sector collaborations between private companies and nonprofit organizations also depend on benefits and inflation.

Ideal partners
According to Firstenberg (1996) and Useem (1987), when it comes to choosing a nonprofit partner, companies tend to focus on *reputation*. Of course, a highly renowned social organization will be more appealing to companies than a less prestigious one. Closely related to reputation, nonprofits' *size* is another feature that companies view as significant: the larger the organization, the more attractive it is for businesses. Also, *geographical proximity* may be crucial. Similarly, a minimum image *compatibility* between potential partners is essential, as well.

When nonprofits approach companies, the quality of the programs proposed is usually a decisive factor, as well as their success potential. Programs including *specific benefits* for companies are more welcomed than those offering implicit or somewhat uncertain benefits. Finally, like in all other human activities, *interpersonal relationships* generally play a significant role in cross-sector agreements.

The Collaboration Continuum

Sustainable collaborations essentially hinge on two factors: *incentives* for both parties to continue collaborating – benefits perceived by partners – and the ability to overcome the problems arising in collaboration *management* (Duronio and Loessin, 1993; Embley, 1993; Austin, 2000; Vernis, 1998b). We have already discussed the benefits that collaborations may provide for organizations, while collaboration management will be dealt with in the following section.

The parameters ruling collaborations are three: time, party commitment and collaboration focus. The former two are paramount and affect the collaboration continuum, whereas the latter, as we shall see, has a lesser relevance (Austin, 2000).

In general, and contrary to expectations, collaborations are not usually broken. Rather, they tend to just conclude. In any case, when collaborations are indeed interrupted, break-up causes are usually associated with *power* conflicts or lack of *trust* (Melendez, 2001; Duronio and Loessin, 1993; Austin, 2000; Vernis, 1998b).

There are many ways to collaborate. Ever more often, collaborations are meant to go beyond mere unilateral donations from companies to social organizations. To that end, we believe it useful to discuss the various inter-action levels produced in collaborations, as well as the process leading to them and how they evolve as partners get to know each other and merge together (Table 2.1).

According to Austin (2000), transactional collaborations are strategic – that is, companies and social organizations join their efforts in the areas where they share common interests. This stage in collaborations clearly implies outgrowing the donations that characterize the philanthropic phase. Finally, few collaborations manage to reach the integrative stage, in which partners become fully integrated. In this phase, collaborations permeate all the areas in partners' operations. Organizations include their collaborations in all their board decisions, from their mission statements to their specific operations.

Table 2.1	The collaboration continuum		
Cross-sector collaboration continuum			
Phase	Philanthropic	Transactional	Integrative
Commitment	Low ▪ ▪ ▪ ⟶		High
Mission significance	Low ▪ ▪ ▪ ⟶		High
Resources	Few ▪ ▪ ▪ ⟶		Plenty
Activities' objectives	Specific ▪ ▪ ▪ ⟶		Broad
Interaction rhythm	Low ▪ ▪ ▪ ⟶		High
Management complexity	Low ▪ ▪ ▪ ⟶		High
Strategic value	Low ▪ ▪ ▪ ⟶		High

Source: Austin, 2000.

Cross-sector collaborations rarely reach the third, more advanced stage. Unfortunately, only very few make it past the philanthropic phase, and fewer still manage to go beyond the transactional stage.

Alliances between organizations often evolve through the collaboration continuum over time in an unplanned fashion. Again, as Austin points out (2001b), contrary to common assumptions, partners do not need to share a specific affinity or similar behavior. When both parties are willing to collaborate, they always find common grounds to undertake their collaboration plans.

Obstacles, Problems and Risks

Currently, several obstacles preclude the development of further collaborations between social organizations and business companies. Which factors generate these obstacles? Why are these opposing forces produced? Among these factors, some are intuitive, while others more unexpected. Next, we shall review some of these obstacles, since, often enough, knowing them helps finding a remedy.

Historical antagonism
The confrontation with some business sub-sectors that has characterized certain nonprofit organizations accounts for some measure of distrust still estranging both sectors. In any case, the third sector currently stands divided in its regard for private businesses. On the one hand, several organizations

are still very critical of the business community – for example, we are all only too aware of the ongoing cry from the most radical environmental organizations against oil companies' environmentally unfriendly policies. On the other hand, many other nonprofits have moved toward a more collaborative approach.

Cultural differences
Organizational cultures in nonprofit and profit organizations differ greatly; these dissimilarities often jeopardize collaborations. For instance, top private business managers resort to a knowledge base, a set of managerial tools and a language that are dramatically different from those used by nonprofits' leaders.

Lack of meeting grounds
There are very few intermediary structures fostering communications and networking between both sectors. Business associations and third-sector coordinators are ill-suited for this task: the former because they have different goals, the latter because they fail to hold a common position with the business sector and, hence, find themselves divided in their approach.

Insufficient resources
As we shall discuss later, economic conditions significantly compromise both sectors' willingness to work together. Private companies tend to be less willing to collaborate with the third sector in times of crisis.

Competition for resources
The dramatic increase in social needs has spearheaded new venues for both sectors: companies have ventured into areas that used to be the realm of the public or third sectors, while social organizations have expanded their operations to areas traditionally held by the public or private sectors.

Problems

Mutual distrust, power unbalances – usually favoring corporations – and *cultural dissimilarities* must be borne in mind, and we shall try to work them out later.

Businesses' impatience for harvesting the fruits of collaborations becomes a problem in many cases, mostly in companies that feature a short-term focus, concentrating on sales or on specific product marketing. This impatience is coupled with the ever-present uncertainty of a more or less precise appraisal of the benefits to be rendered by collaboration ventures. In addition, nonprofits also often succumb to impatience and a short-term mindset when they are overly focused on fund-raising.

It should also be noted that some corporations still adhere to what Goldberg defines as "schizophrenic" attitudes (Goldberg, 1990), combining ventures to collaborate with civil society with their efforts to lobby for some of their own interests that are highly detrimental to society at large. This phenomenon will only vanish when corporations become truly and deeply committed to civil society issues. Nonprofits also fall prey to contradictory behaviors. Often, their denounce or awareness-raising campaigns clash with their fund-raising operations, yielding to a schizophrenia of their own.

Finally, we should look into an existing *paradox*: companies engage more in cross-sector collaborations when business is booming, while their support to nonprofit organizations dwindles considerably during critical times, when in fact their contributions are more necessary (Goldberg, 1990). To offset this phenomenon, the third sector should try to achieve and maintain financial independence, enhancing its ability to cope with reduced corporate support.

Risks

Nonprofits should avoid the risk entailed by neglecting their mission to satisfy the demands of supporting companies. Growing dependent on businesses and their contributions may cause this undesired effect. Financial dependence on public administrations may produce a similar problem. In both cases, financial independence tends to be a suitable antidote. To ensure financial independence, social organizations need to diversify and optimize their current funding sources as well as exploit potential alternative sources. Straying from their missions may also result from "organizational isomorphism", as defined by Smith (1989) – that is, due to uneven power balance and excessive dependence, nonprofits may end up absorbing their sponsors' mindset, culture and approach.

The use of social organizations' image to boost company or product performance may imply severe risks. First, target audiences should be carefully considered. Some promotional campaigns may be acceptable when they are addressed to an educated audience and detrimental for less educated segments. Also, messages should be carefully analyzed. It is also necessary to exercise additional caution when civil society organizations grant the exclusive use of their image to a single company.

Smaller social organizations or those advocating less popular causes may face greater risks in this collaboration boom. Since these nonprofits hold very little appeal for businesses, they may easily be left out and deprived of potential benefits. Mergers may provide a solution, although they are not always desirable or convenient. Another possibility lies in the creation of intermediate structures, such as associations gathering several nonprofit organizations to enhance their appeal for companies interested in collaborations (see Chapter 4). This option may prove inconvenient in the future, since companies prefer to be free to choose the social organizations that best respond to their own interests. Therefore, some of the less corporately "attractive" nonprofits run the risk of extinction, along with the services they provide.

In addition, the ongoing changes currently experienced by both nonprofit and business organizations may prevent cross-sector relationships to mature adequately.

Collaboration Forms and Structures

Collaborations are defined according to the structure and format they adopt. Communication and coordination channels, in turn, are determined by structure – which may be a joint platform, a network, a parallel organization, an agreement setting the guidelines for interactions or an informal alliance. Next, we will analyze some of the specific structures used by companies to pursue collaborations: corporate foundations, social investment funds and other five formats.

Corporate Foundations

Some companies prefer to undertake their sponsorships through a corporate foundation. In fact, corporate foundations are created, first, to centralize contributions and optimize their profitability. Contributions made through foundations are not only more visible but also easier to deduce from taxes. Second, foundations also act as a buffer between social assistance and companies, making contributions more reliable and independent. This distance allows corporate foundations to develop long-term commitments. Still, corporate foundations do not usually engulf the entire assistance scope offered by companies (Ruyra de Andrade and Sotelo-Zuloaga Galdiz, 1999). Regrettably, many corporate foundations do not fully and strategically align their operations with those of their parent companies.

Cause-related Marketing

The first collaboration between a nonprofit organization and a business company built on cause-related marketing was undertaken by American Express in the early 1980s to fund the restoration of several public monuments (Maru File and Prince, 1995). In this type of collaboration, a company promotes a product through the image of a social issue, donating part of its revenues to it.[1]

For companies, this kind of collaboration enhances the image of one of their products or the company as a whole. Thus, results are measured in terms of not only boosted popularity but also increased revenues. For social organizations, cause marketing implies an increased support for one of its operations, greater awareness for this issue and new potential revenue sources. Cause marketing features an added advantage: it makes it easy for consumers to get involved with a social issue. Simply by satisfying their own needs, consumers may contribute to a cause they sympathize with. Companies' approach to cause marketing has evolved from a short-term, sales-oriented focus to a long-term commitment intended to boost corporate image. This method is highly appealing to companies. In fact, in the United States, for example, 89 percent of consumers value socially responsible companies (Independent Sector, 2001), while two-thirds of all consumers are willing to switch brands to promote worthy causes (Yankey, 1996). Another attractive feature in this type of collaborations is that benefits are obvious and allow companies to allocate marketing funds to social activities.

When it comes to seeking partners for cause marketing campaigns, companies first focus on the social sector they are targeting. Then, they look for a cause as closely related to their core business as possible. Finally, they need to make sure the cause they have chosen is appealing to their target segment. Companies select nonprofits very carefully before supporting them. They shun inconsistent, inappropriate and controversial potential partners. In some cases, companies have gone as far as creating and launching their own social projects.

The risks entailed by cause marketing and the criticism elicited refer to the fact that these actions raise funds for popular causes needing very little support, while they avert less popular and marketable issues. In addition, there is the fear that nonprofits become market-oriented, losing their altruistic and social nature. Finally, cause marketing campaigns may produce a negative effect: under the impression that the cause is receiving enough attention, other donors may reduce their contributions to it.

Sponsorship and Donations

Collaborations based on sponsorships or donations – the former implies advertising, whereas the latter refers to "pure" philanthropy – encompass any kind of support provided by companies to nonprofit organizations. Corporate support may take the form of in-kind contributions – new or used materials – or cash donations – unilaterally or through the practice of "matching funds" contributed by employees.[2] Companies may also lend their premises or provide logistic support to nonprofits. Corporate support may be provided directly by companies or through their corporate foundations.

American Express and the World Monument Watch

In 1995, American Express funded an ambitious five-year plan for the nonprofit World Monument Fund to carry out a survey of the world's greatest monuments and sites in imperiled state (www.worldmonuments.org). In 2000, American Express renewed its commitment for an additional five-year period. According to Bonnie Burnham, WMF chair, collaborating with American Express has provided financial support and an enhanced image for this initiative. The company's reputation has made it easier for this nonprofit to work with beneficiaries and local public administrations involved (American Express, 2000, http://home3.americanexpress.com/corp/gb/wmf.asp).

Increasingly often, companies incorporate collaborations to their marketing strategies and mission statements. As far as companies are concerned, sponsorship or patronage programs offer a great potential for image enhancement and a means to exercise their social responsibility. For nonprofits, instead, these collaborations provide material or financial assistance. The most relevant risk entailed in these kinds of collaborations is the so-called *boomerang effect*: damages to the reputation of one of the organizations may affect both of them.

Employee Volunteers

In this type of collaboration, companies lend their manpower to nonprofit organizations. Nonprofits may require the advice of specialized company employees to improve their operations and train their personnel – for example, a marketing or accounting expert. Similarly, companies may offer some of their employees to carry out required tasks for nonprofits. These collaborations have increased considerably over recent years (Yankey, 1996).

The chance to borrow corporate manpower may hold a great appeal for small and medium-sized organizations. Smaller nonprofits often lack the necessary or qualified personnel to undertake their operations adequately. For companies, this option provides enhanced motivation potential for employees. Volunteer activities afford an additional sense of usefulness for employees, boosting their motivation.

These collaborations may sprout from companies' top management to encourage employees and present them with new scenarios. However, volunteer initiatives may also arise among employees themselves. In this case, companies try to funnel employees' desires by seeking a suitable nonprofit to exploit volunteer work.

Service Purchases

A rather widespread collaboration practice involves the purchase of services provided by nonprofit organizations. Usually, companies incur no additional expenses, for example, when they hire a group of mentally handicapped individuals to tend to their garden areas.

Supplying products or services offers nonprofits an opportunity to develop new funding sources, as opposed to seeking sponsorships, which merely substitutes one financial source – public funding, for instance – for another – corporate support. Nonprofits' revenues from service sales have increased considerably over the past 20 years (The Aspen Institute, 2001).

Like all other collaboration forms, service sales also imply risks for nonprofits, including the interruption of service supply to needy sectors, nonprofits' neglect for "unmarketable" services, a reduction of volunteer work and potential internal conflicts arising between nonprofits' pro-revenue and pro-cause members.

Others: Accreditation, Licenses and Microcredits for Nonprofits

Social sector organizations may certify companies or help set accreditation standards for other granting firms or organizations. Companies apply and pay for accreditation in order to prove and advertise their civil responsibility – for example, as environmentally friendly organizations.

There are four types of accreditations: those issued by companies themselves, second-party accreditations issued by industry or sector associations, third-party accreditations issued by outside sources, such as nonprofits, and those issued by international agencies. Needless to say, certifications issued by third parties – especially nonprofits – carry more credibility than those issued by companies themselves (Gereffi, Garcia-Johnson, Sasser, 2001).[3]

Certifications

The Social Accountability International (SAI) organization has devised a certification system for sustainable development companies – the SA8000 standard. Numerous companies have been involved in this development, which also called for three rounds of workshops to adjust required standards. This organization also offers training and consultancy services for companies (www.cepaa.org).

Social sector organizations may also grant licenses for products complying with specific standards – for example, products suitable for individuals suffering from diabetes, high cholesterol or blood pressure levels.

In addition to the above-mentioned collaboration practices, financial institutions also rely on other structures to collaborate with the third sector, such as the *microcredits for nonprofits*. These funds offer loans to nonprofits at special rates, below market values. These institutions are paramount, since moderate indebtedness is currently an unavoidable strategy for all kinds of organizations, including nonprofits. These banks were created to respond to the financial problems typically experienced by nonprofits, particularly those undertaking publicly funded projects, which usually only receive a minimum advanced payment. Traditionally, nonprofits bump into several obstacles in this regard, including limited access to capital markets, discriminatory treatment as compared to for-profit organizations, long-term loan unavailability, unaffordable variable interest rates and exposure to potential loan withdrawal. In addition, small- and medium-sized nonprofits also find it very hard to manage their own financial situation. These specific hindrances add to the mutual distrust ingrained in both the financial and the nonprofit sectors. Still, nonprofits should analyze their debt strategy very carefully.

Forest Stewardship Council

Since 1993, the social organization called Forest Stewardship Council (FSC) operates an accreditation program for wood industry companies proving to adhere to responsible forest management practices. This organization has separated certification standard issuance from certification bodies in an attempt to preserve their independence. The FSC does not issue certifications or accept donations directly from companies. An intermediary foundation receives donations for the FSC (www.fscoax.org).

Information

Both internal and external information are crucial for successful collaborations. Especially in high-profile collaborations, both organizations should know each other thoroughly in order to learn what to offer and what to expect in return. In other words, organizations need to share a single identity, embraced by all their members. The knowledge of one's own organizational culture and identity plays a crucial role in collaboration processes, since organizations' ability to cooperate depends on their cultural and goal compatibility. Thus, vision and mission clarity and knowledge constitute basic requirements.

Communications

Closely related to information, communications are a key ingredient in cross-sector collaborations between nonprofits and business companies. Sara Meléndez, *Independent Sector* principal until recently, defines communications as a pillar for successful collaborations (Meléndez, 2001). Once civil organizations have accurate information on their own operations and objectives, communications will flow easily to support cross-sector interactions devoid of misunderstandings and distrust.

Indeed, given the mutual mistrust and ignorance between nonprofits and companies, good communications are invaluable. The communication effort required in cross-sector collaborations is similar to that used by companies and nonprofits when they initiate operations in markets or countries that are new to them. Cultural dissimilarities call for a greater communication zeal to endure a long and often slow task. However, in the long run, communications reduce transaction costs. In addition, communications will also enable nonprofits to ensure an egalitarian treatment, since companies tend to build unequal relationships, based on the mistaken premise that "money rules". As regards communications between companies and nonprofits, public administrations may play a decisive intermediary role.

Also, consultants may act as buffers, assisting inexperienced nonprofits in cross-sector collaborations.

The need to encourage fluent and clear communications should apply not only to partners, but also to their outside stakeholders. Some social sectors, especially in Continental Europe, are still rather suspicious of collaborations between the business and nonprofit sectors. Thus, it is necessary to bolster collaborations' credibility and to dispel remaining taboos. To that end, communication plans must be drawn to enhance and expose both collaboration projects and collaborations themselves.

Additionally, communications are not only crucial for cross-sector collaboration processes. All social organizations should make significant communication efforts even before building collaborations, since they need to make themselves known to the business sector, displaying their features and potential contributions to companies. In fact, many private companies – especially small ones – still ignore the potential benefits of collaborating with nonprofit organizations.

Evaluation

Strong, long-lasting and transparent relationships demand the evaluation of collaboration results. Yet, to assess collaborations, clear expectations must be set before initiating collaborations. Evaluations will depend on the drivers that led organizations to collaborate and on expected results. Thus, for companies, collaborations will be measured in terms of revenue increases, market share growth, distributors' response, personnel commitment to projects, top management's attitudes, relationships with social partners, expenses and benefits. In turn, nonprofits will assess the support provided by society as a result of collaborations, as well as the specific support received from companies and projects' exposure.

However, cross-sector collaborations between the business and nonprofit sectors should always be measured according to a double standard, registering both the benefits for partner organizations as well as the benefits for society at large.

Efficient management and professionalism

Professionalism and management capabilities are basic components in any sound collaboration. This does not mean that social organizations should increase their work load, but that their operations should be professionally carried out and well managed. This requirement applies especially to less professionalized or experienced nonprofits. Many companies collaborating with nonprofits feature a significant size, great visibility and intensive work rhythm. Professional and managerial dissimilarities may affect collaborations.

Therefore, these factors should be borne in mind when nonprofits agree to perform specific tasks.

Often enough, companies behave quite unprofessionally, particularly those using collaborations as mere marketing techniques. Nevertheless, it should be noted that, frequently, companies have a greater management capability, which may lead to frictions and dissatisfaction.

To improve their internal and collaboration management skills, nonprofits should incorporate some of the working methods used by businesses. Although they have enhanced their effectiveness, many nonprofits still need to work hard on this area, since collaborations may unveil and emphasize their managerial shortcomings. In fact, as we have mentioned before, collaborations provide an outstanding opportunity to absorb the new techniques used by business companies. Many nonprofits have exploited this opportunity in the areas of finances, marketing and project management.

Specifically, adequate management for unique organizational features calls for the appointment of qualified and experienced individuals who have managed and worked in multicultural, diversified projects. Transparence and accountability are also significant factors, both for management and for trust-building tasks. For example, nonprofits should incorporate management performance measurements. Collaboration leaders should also be able to guarantee consistency and to manage motivation, change, commitment and self-regulation. Self-regulating skills are paramount, since in collaborations between deeply different organizations, a balanced exchange is crucial.

Task division and assignment must be carried out jointly and focusing on value creation potential. In other words, each organization should zero in on what it does best. Also of utmost importance is setting quality, transparence and performance standards. Adequate standards and task allocations will pave the way to collaboration success.

CHAPTER 3

Collaborations Between Public Administrations and Nonprofits: Towards a Relational Society

Introduction

Since the late 1980s, as a result of the problems in the welfare State, we have witnessed a significant shift in the social and political attitudes associated with the public sector in virtually all OECD countries (Prats, 2000). Along with the environment changes described in the introduction to the first section of this book, two other phenomena also stand out. First, the classic State funding model has experienced a severe crisis, which has translated into widespread budgetary emergency and has driven administrations to seek new paths for efficiency improvements. Second, governmental legitimacy has also become profoundly questioned. The State is still perceived as necessary, but it has ceased to be viewed as the foremost driver in economic and social transformations. In other words, governments no longer have all the answers to all the problems, on account of their nature and complexity. Actually, now there are multiple agents that should be taken into account for the search for and development of solutions to the challenges faced by current societies. This is what some analysts have defined as "welfare pluralism".

As a result of this paradigm change, which has led the public sector to a thorough redefinition of roles, as revealed by public policy bibliography and practice, there has been a quantitative and qualitative increase in cross-sector collaborations between public administrations and nonprofit organizations. On the one hand, for the public sector, nonprofits, on account of their specificity, are able to provide specific responses to the new social demands. On the other, as we shall discuss throughout this chapter, administrations often resort to nonprofits to outsource public services in order to address oversize and bureaucratic inefficiency issues. Such is the case, for instance, of a public development cooperation agency that decides to channel its projects through a Northern NGO in collaboration with a Southern counterpart, or the case of a public agency for housing relief that retains a social NGO to assist the homeless.

The Relational State

The very limitations exhibited by the welfare State to respond to the demands of an increasingly developed, complex and interdependent society, emphasized by the pressures derived from economic internationalization, clearly expose the need to reformulate the relationships between the public and private sectors, between State and society, yielding to the emergence of a relational State. (Mendoza, 1991)

A rising number of signs are starting to reveal that the public–private dichotomy is fading away, while the relevance and value of the "non-state public" notion (Bresser and Cunill, 1998)[1] become more and more popular. Increasing public administration support for the third sector does not mean a lesser State; it does not imply that the welfare State is being "privatized". On the contrary, the State is going "public" (Bresser, 1997; Giddens, 2000). It should be clear that the "public realm" must not be identified exclusively with public administrations, that many of the activities undertaken by social organizations are indeed "public" and, hence, collaborations between public administrations and third-sector organizations should not be named as "privatizations".

Opponents to an increased involvement of nonprofits in social services argue that the "public service spirit" is corrupted when social services are not provided by public organizations. It is true that the dedication of most public administration workers stems from their commitment to society. Still, we should not forget that public administration employees are not the only ones building a community service spirit; the great majority of social organization workers also share the same spirit. Bresser (1997:43) takes this concept a step further and puts it as follows: "In any case, it should be noted that the single most significant reason for turning to nonprofits is not because they are more efficient in service supply than any other institution, but because they undertake roles that neither the State nor the market can perform. And, as reliability, dedication and solidarity account for the specific features differentiating the nonprofit from the profit sector, flexibility, specialized experience availability and the ability to reach out to unaccesible customers are portrayed as some of the greatest advantages the nonprofit sector can offer as compared to the public sector."

Why Is There a Relationship Between Public Administrations and Nonprofits?

Some of the drivers fueling public–private collaborations have already been discussed. However, as expressed by one of the leading third-sector scholars, Professor Lester Salamon (1995), this question has more than a single answer. Salamon and Anheier (1998)[2] state that several theories combined favor the development of public–private relationships.

The Welfare State

The first theory reviewed by Salamon is the *theory of the welfare State*. This theory grants a highly significant role to public administrations and undermines the relevance of the private nonprofit sector. As Salamon points out, this notion is not currently useful, since, although the State has indeed withheld its exclusive power to formulate public policies, it has not done so in public policy implementation – a field in which public agencies collaborate intensely with the nonprofit private sector. As we shall see later, the welfare State theory has been outdated by the theory of the relational State (Mendoza, 1991) and/or the welfare pluralism theory (Taylor, 1990).

The Government Failure

The second theory, entitled the *government failure*, explains the emergence of nonprofit organizations as a result of public agency failure. Specifically, this theory argues that governments' collective good production "will generally produce a level of services that will exceed what some voters demand and fall short of what others request" (Weisbrod, 1988). As a result, private nonprofits will try to meet unsatisfied demands. In short, this theory views nonprofit organizations as substitutes for public agencies. In any case, it does not provide a suitable framework to study public–private relationships, since it cannot anticipate whether governments will want to retain nonprofits for the delivery of certain public services (Smith and Lipsky, 1993).

The Contract Failure

The third theory, known as *the contract failure*, accounts for volunteer organizations by means of the trust clients/users/donors place in them. Customer trust results from the fact that, in many public services, it is very hard to gather information on supply quality and quantity, thus making it nearly impossible to assess whether services are adequately provided. On these grounds, service recipients consider nonprofits as worthier of their trust (Hansmann, 1987). However, customer trust does not explain why public agencies hire nonprofits, since public organizations are even less expected to betray their users' trust and are heavily regulated to prevent such occurrence (Salamon, 1995; Smith and Lipsky, 1993).

Third-sector Governance

Still unsatisfied by these theories, Salamon has developed two others to try to explain public–private collaborations. The first of his theories, called *third-sector governance*, basically states that public agencies are using private agencies to "perform government tasks". In this type of relationships, governments set general guidelines, but nonprofits are free to deliver programs as they see fit. In fact, some of these organizations are older than public administrations and supplement public sector's tasks. Hence, it does not seem logical for public administrations to entrust them with certain activities.

Nonprofit Failure

The second theory developed by Salamon, known as *voluntary failure*, explains public–private collaborations as governmental interventions to correct the wrongdoings of the nonprofit or volunteer sector. Thus, this theory justifies State intervention on account of third-sector imperfections. Salamon identifies four nonprofit sector failures:

1. *Insufficiency*: Nonprofit organizations are unable to provide the necessary resources to solve some of the issues in modern societies.
2. *Particularism*: Many nonprofits focus their activities on some population segments, completely neglecting others.

3. *Paternalism*: Community needs are frequently defined by its more affluent members instead of by the community itself.
4. *Amateurism*: Oftentimes, nonprofits fail to attract good professionals to help them solve their problems.

Welfare Pluralism

Although these latter two theories – *third-sector governance* and *volunteer failure* – do make very interesting contributions to the public–private relation debate, in our opinion, their explanations seem rather restricted to the US scenario and are only partially applicable in Europe, on account of its history and idiosyncrasies. The most salient difficulty lies in the fact that both theories disregard the prevailing role played by political institutions in specifying the nature of the nonprofit sector.

At this point, it may be helpful to discuss the *welfare pluralis*m theory or the "relational State" model (Mendoza, 1991) we mentioned at the introduction. Hatch and Mocroft (1983) approach this theory in the following manner: "It may be used to express the fact that social and sanitary services may be provided by four sectors: the public, the volunteer, the market and the informal sectors. Specifically, welfare pluralism implies that the State currently plays a less dominant role and does not view itself as the only possible instrument to supply collective welfare social services." Mendoza (1995) suggests that the starting point of the relational State lies in "the recognition that the State has ceased to be – if indeed it ever was – almighty and self-sufficient" – a State "that acknowledges the current complexity and interdependence of social problems and understands that their solutions may only be approached through the active collaboration of society itself" (1995: 11).

Lenox Hill Neighborhood House

This nonprofit organization based in New York originated as a day-care center in 1894, and, nowadays, it yearly assists over 20,000 people who live, work or attend school in Manhattan's Upper East Side. It provides support to children, entire families, and homeless, needy or elderly people. Half its funding comes from private contributions (individual donations, foundations, companies, etc.) and the other half, from collaborations with several departments of New York's city administration, as well as from contributions from the federal and state administrations.

Evers (1993) refers to this theory as "the notion of the welfare mix" and assigns to nonprofits an intermediary position among markets, governments and families. According to this author, the third sector should be mapped without clearly defined boundaries, since it holds a position where "different rationales and standards seamlessly merge and overlap." As we discussed in our introductory chapter, the core idea denotes that nonprofit organizations hold an intermediate position as regards three kinds of relationships: those built between the market and public interest, between universal states and specific nonprofits, and between nonprofits and the informal sector, consisting of families, friends and communities. Third-sector organizations are hybrids, that may occasionally produce services outsourced by public administrations, thus adopting a public nature, or may stand up for the rights of society at large or of an individual segment, assuming a community purpose, or may collaborate with business companies to raise funds and pursue a more market-oriented stance.

Fifteen years before, in the United States, Berger and Neuhaus (1977) anticipated the notions eventually presented by Evers. They coined the term "mediating structures" to refer to nonprofit organizations, defined as institutions located halfway between individuals and public agencies.

Why do Public Administrations Collaborate?

As we said in the introduction, the so-called public service outsourcing has become a viable option to solve the bureaucratic inefficiency and oversize problems affecting public agencies in modern States. Upon discussing public service outsourcing, we should discern between two clearly distinctive public agency tasks that are usually confounded: provision and production (Kolderie, 1986). Public service provision entails a political decision to provide – or not – any given service, to establish offering contents, to assign public resources to fund it and to set service access conditions. It implies several activities, such as regulation, acquisition, funding, planning and so on. Production, instead, refers to the technical and organizational process involved in service provision. Thus, the point here is to determine whether public agencies will produce the service or services they have already decided to provide – in other words, if they are going to sell, run, manage, control and assess these services.

Certainly, each provision and production activity may be divided into several parts to be outsourced separately. In simple terms, this distinction between provision and production allows for the categorization, as well, of the four areas shown in Table 3.1 (Kolderie, 1986):

Table 3.1	Division between provision and production		
		Production	
		Private	**Public**
Provision	Private	Private sector	Public sector selling to the private sector
	Public	Outsourcing	Public sector

Recently, several authors have stated that, in order for cross-sector collaborations between the public and private sector to exist, the former must join the market logics. For example, Hirschman (1992) has explained the application of its well-known *exit-voice* mechanism (Hirschman, 1970) to public services. The author argues that, in the production of most public services, there is no "market discipline", and he pleads for the introduction of some form of "market pressure" to ensure productivity and service quality.

In a series of studies on public management, the OECD uses the expression "market mechanisms" to refer to management instruments introducing, at least, a single market feature – be it competition, price, monetary incentives

Table 3.2	Arguments for public–private collaborations			
Approach ↓	**Function**			
	Provision			**Production**
	Funding	**Regulation and planning**	**Control and evaluation**	
Welfare State	Public administrations	Public administrations	Public administrations	Public administrations with occasional third-sector support
Welfare pluralism	Public administrations with co-funding from individuals and support from business companies	Governments, third sector and business companies	Public administrations with third-sector collaboration	Third sector and business companies
Neoliberalism	Private sources	Market	Market	Private companies with third-sector security contributions

or so on. These instruments include outsourcing, cross-government cooperation, franchising and licenses, subsidies, regulating coupons and users' payments. In its research on alternative service supply systems, the United States' International City Management Association (ICMA) also cites these mechanisms as the most widely spread among US domestic public agencies (Valente and Manchester, 1984). However, when it comes to using these mechanisms, countries find their own individual ways to do so.

Finally, the Table 3.2 may prove helpful to understand cross-sector collaborations involving public administrations and nonprofits against the backdrop of welfare pluralism and on the basis of the distinction between production and provision.

The Collaboration Continuum and Public–private Collaboration Forms

Kramer (1981), a pioneer in the study of the relationships between the nonprofit and the public sectors, upholds that these cross-sector relations are not static and may adopt five basic forms, depending on prevailing economic policies: re-privatization, strengthening, pragmatic association, subordination to the State and nationalization. In short, public–private relationships fall into a continuum that spans from a system dominated by private organizations, solely seeking economic benefits by providing services to society and gradually substituting for nonprofits (re-privatization), to a system in which the State runs everything (nationalization) and nonprofits have a marginal role (Table 3.3).

We are particularly interested in the three relationship forms located at the center of the public–private sequence, which may also be referred to as "market pluralism", "welfare pluralism" and "welfare State". In the first form, "third-sector strengthening", nonprofits would be reinforced and could substitute for public agencies. In the second case, "collaborative partnership", public agencies and private organizations cooperate and complement each other. In the third instance, nonprofits are viewed almost as a hindrance and should surrender to the State.

Although all these "market instruments" imply a "relation" between public and private sectors, the outsourcing formula has been the most proficient in its use of words such as "collaboration" or "partnership" – surely because this is the most widely exploited instrument in all countries and the one demanding a closer bond between public agencies and private organizations. In OECD countries, outsourcing has become one of

Table 3.3 Public–private collaboration continuum				
Re-privatization	**Third-sector strengthening**	**Pragmatic partnership**	**Subordination to the State**	**Nationalization**
Private companies increasingly seize "public" areas	Social sector organizations increasingly seize "public" areas	Social sector organizations collaborate with and complement public agencies	Social sector organizations report to the State	The State increasingly seizes civil society areas
Business market	Market pluralism	Welfare pluralism	Welfare State	Public market
PRIVATE ◀━━━━━━━━━━━━━━━━━━━━━━━▶ PUBLIC				

Source: Elaborated by authors, based on Kramer (1981), Taylor (1990) and Wolch (1990).

the most widespread forms of public–private interactions in public services and takes several formats. Depending on their operating area – national, regional, local – public agencies and nonprofits favor some outsourcing forms or others. Similarly, services produced are also more suited for some outsourcing forms than others. Table 3.4 summarizes all major outsourcing forms.

Table 3.4 Major outsourcing forms				
Ownership	**Management**	**Funding**	**Human Resources**	**Description (example)**
Public	Private	Public	Public	Management contract (hiring a private organization to manage a public home)
Public	Private	Public	Private	Management and operation contract (hiring a private organization to manage a public home, using the private organization's personnel)
Public	Public	Public	Private and Public	Operation contract (temporarily hiring an association's monitors for some municipal camps at the City Hall's social service center)
Private	Public	Private and Public	Private	Public equipment and premise rentals (renting city premises for an association's camp activities)

Private	Private	Private and Public	Public and Private	Public workers assigned to a private organization (training program delivered by public instructors at an association)
Private	Private	Public and Private	Private	Subsidy or agreement (internal training program funded by a public administration and delivered by association's trainers)

Source: Elaborated by authors on the basis of Savas, 1987.

Problems in Collaboration

There are two core issues to be considered in this type of collaborations. First, how should nonprofits' undeniable desire to perverse their autonomy be reconciled with public agencies' legitimate need to control public fund spending? Second, how should the demand for public action to evenly reach everyone (universalism) match social organizations' urge to serve specific targets (specificity)? No magic trick may provide an answer to either question.

Professor James (1983) warns that nonprofits could jeopardize their demand for autonomy by providing the services desired by their principals. James argues that, like any sound professional, social organization leaders try to offer the services that ensure their prestige, satisfaction or professional reward. Gilbert (1985) and Kramer (1985), among other authors, also report on a problem associated with the second issue mentioned above. These cross-sector collaborations may yield a two-tiered social service system, consisting of a first tier, managed by nonprofits, providing services for less in need people, and a second tier, under the responsibility of public agencies, responding to the needs of those individuals nonprofits refuse to serve.

Thus, public and nonprofit practitioners would have to strive to find a delicate balance between autonomy and control, on the one hand, and between universalism and specificity, on the other. If we dig deeper into this subject and carefully review current bibliography on public–private collaboration, we find that the list of problems deriving from it is not restricted to the two core issues we have described. To further enable our discussion, we have classified these problems into four categories: lack of flexibility, funding, human resources and quality.

Lack of Flexibility

A twofold *lack of flexibility* is clearly detected. First, these collaborations cause systems to lack diversity. For a nonprofit public service system to work, public agencies need nonprofit organizations to meet several requirements that are meant to ensure nonprofits' standardization. Naturally, although most nonprofits are becoming increasingly similar, the system tends to be deprived of flexibility. Second, collaborations make it hard for changes to be introduced. Both parties want service supply to change as little as possible in order to avoid plunging into an unknown territory, where the collaboration itself may be endangered. Thus, new ideas for service improvements are unlikely to be introduced and fostered. Summing up, public–private collaborations might end up building a rigid and bureaucratic social service system that is far removed from its original goals.

Additionally, legal guidelines and regulations (public contract standards) also pose some quite remarkable problems for public–private relationships. Indeed, public contracts – designed for scenarios where contract purposes must be accurately defined, long-lasting stability, as well as a consolidated market, is a given, and relationships are based on control rather than mutual trust or learning – do not seem altogether suitable to set the ground rules for public–private collaborations.

The Cotonou Agreement

One of the innovations featured by the Cotonou Agreement – ruling the interactions between European Union and African, Caribbean and Pacific (ACP) States since June 2000 – lies in its explicit recognition of the complementary – yet fundamental – role played by civil society, the private sector and decentralized communities, along with the States, in the development and cooperation process.

The definition of domestic development strategies is still a responsibility of ACP governments, but non-State actors must be, for the first time ever, involved throughout the entire process. In this regard, the agreement includes highly innovating guidelines to promote engagement approaches that allow for non-State actors to participate, such as mandatory reporting to these actors in order to provide them with adequate information on the agreement and its application, necessary inclusion of these actors in political debates regarding EU–ACP cooperation, as well as in the programs and projects undertaken, and support for these actors to secure their institutional strengthening.

However, these guidelines are difficult to implement, considering the stringent legal framework (European Development Fund – FED – by-laws) that regulates EU–ACP interactions as regards public–private contracting. Crucial aspects, such as institutional strengthening and cross-actor collaboration or support, do not fit in with FED's dispositions.

Funding

Several problems arise when we talk about *funding*. First, in many Western democracies, nonprofit organizations/associations are becoming increasingly dependent on public funding. Of course, this dependence is highly hazardous for collaborations because they eventually turn into a "lifeline": if public agencies withdraw their funding, nonprofits are severely endangered. Second, simultaneously, public administrations are currently subject to widespread budgetary restrictions, massively embracing the command to "do more with less money". This situation fuels frustration on both sides: there is very little social service public managers can do to enhance productivity, while nonprofit practitioners are not willing to take less resources after the sector's recent growth. Financial problems do not stop here. Often enough, to secure a contract, social organizations offer their services at very low fees and, if they are indeed awarded the contract, find themselves providing services at below cost. Finally, depending on time-restricted fund allocations spurs uncertainty and rigidity in collaborations.

Human Resources

Public–private collaborations also breed difficulties for *human resources* in both public agencies and nonprofit organizations. On the one hand, once they stopped delivering services and are estranged from customers or users, public sector employees are deprived of a motivation driver in social services – direct contact with beneficiaries. On the other hand, people working at nonprofits are forced to devote what they perceive as an excessive amount of time to coordinating their activities with public administrations. Certainly, the administrative aspects of outsourcing ventures may turn out to be quite discouraging. In addition, social organization workers could lose their inherent altruistic attitude, which in service supply account for a significant advantage over public or private business employees. This altruistic attitude is highly valued as a distinctive feature that renders nonprofits fit to deliver social services – ideally characterized by a selfless personal relationship with users. Studies on this topic also point out that service outsourcing may jeopardize the trust bond built between nonprofits' workers and public agencies, which is, unquestionably, of great relevance to overall social service systems.

Accountability and Quality

From the viewpoint of service *quality*, two major problems plague public–private collaborations. In the first place, traditionally, cross-sector cooperations between public and private entities have not emphasized the notion of quality; currently, it is harder to introduce this key service delivery factor. For instance, result assessment is not customary in services provided by social organizations. In the second place, users'/customers' inputs are usually ignored. If beneficiary satisfaction has been a difficult concept to introduce in social service delivery, outsourcing renders this task even harder.

Collaboration Management

Public and private agents have come to recognize that public administrations and third-sector organizations need to collaborate in order to effectively serve society. However, as may clearly be demonstrated by daily practice in public–private interactions, collaborations are rarely truly managed. It is necessary to reflect further on these relationships and understand that all collaborations must be managed thoroughly. Nowadays, public–private collaboration management is generally limited to submitting programs to win contracts, and, once contracts are awarded, expense reports are submitted upon service completion. "Managed" public–private collaborations would incorporate, at least, *mutual knowledge* and *transparent accounting*. Mutual knowledge means understanding each other's role in the relationship and helping each other perform that role as effectively as possible to achieve a single goal – ensuring the best results for citizens. Transparent reporting should come before parties' individual interests. At the same time, two-way communications should also flow fluently between parties.

Problem Management in Collaborations

The aforementioned concerns regarding flexibility, human resources, funding and quality in cross-sector collaborations between public agencies and nonprofit organizations should be addressed. Here are some remedy proposals:

Flexibility
It goes without saying that, for public–private collaborations to become easier to manage, large organizations developing several activities and

featuring the ability to mobilize resources seem better equipped and suited. This preference is supported on the following grounds:

- First, the larger the organization, the more skilled it is to mobilize several stakeholders at once in order to obtain more economic resources and additional volunteer manpower.
- Second, diverse service offerings enable organizations to transfer experiences from one area to another, broadening their learning opportunities. At the same time, organizations with multiple service offerings are able to supply an overall service package for specific users.
- Third, public dependence is diversified by outsourcing with several public administrations or departments within a single administration.
- Fourth, since these organizations are not focused on a single population segment, innovation and segment exchanges are feasible. For instance, nonprofits working with the elderly tend to incorporate cross-generation programs as well.
- Finally, taking into account that the labor-intensive services offered by nonprofits are numerous, there are no economies of scale in service production. Still, economies of scale may be attained in several production support services, such as accounting, personnel management, marketing, communication, fund-raising and so on.[3]

Funding
It should be noted that public administrations' financial dependence will always be a fairly constant feature, regardless of whether nonprofits or private companies produce social services or not, and that their financial dependence does not necessarily entail a problem for public–private collaboration management. Public managers should be able to analyze the additional value to be contributed by nonprofits in social service outsourcing. Here are some examples to illustrate this point:

- Nonprofit organizations can mobilize *additional human resources* – volunteers – to expand the specific service schedule set by the contract with outsourcing public administrations. For instance, volunteers may account for a very significant support in home assistance services.
- Nonprofits can mobilize *additional economic resources* to add to the public resources allocated to service delivery – for example, donations from individuals and companies.
- Users may be more inclined to accept service co-payment and co-production options if the outsourcing organization is a nonprofit. Users find it easier to relate to the solidarity and justice values driving most nonprofits than to the economic-oriented rationale of private business companies.

Human resources

Informal relationships between public and nonprofit workers smooth collaborations. Therefore, it would be important to provide the necessary means for both groups to meet and bond – for instance, through the organization of seminars, lectures, joint meetings and so on. Additionally, continued exchanges between professionals from both sectors also foster easier working relationships later.

High turnover among public workers, resulting from the successive turnarounds typically undergone by public administrations, clearly hinders public–private relations. Preventing this problem escapes both public and nonprofit managers – forever and unwillingly trapped in politicians' see-saw maneuvers. However, perhaps the creation of specialized public service units will improve public–private relationships. For instance, a specific unit could be created to collect service information and experiences and to serve as a liaison with outsourcing organizations.

An Approach to a "Decalogue" for Collaborations between Public Administrations and Nonprofit Organizations

- At both ends, political and technical leaders shall be *willing* to work together.
- Both parties shall have a *real need* to collaborate, and the result of this collaboration shall be the creation of *public value*.
- Both collaborating organizations shall build *mutual knowledge* (as to their limitations, expectations, etc.).
- Collaborations shall be ensured through planning and resources.
- *Common goals* shall be set, contemplating living condition improvements for users/beneficiaries.
- *Transparent mechanisms* shall be set in place to monitor, control and evaluate collaborations.
- Potential collaboration hindrances shall be anticipated to enable both parties to work on *alternative solutions*.
- Network results shall be *jointly* and continuously *assessed*.
- Whenever necessary, both parties shall analyze *new collaboration structures* or develop existing structures innovatively.
- *Human resources efforts* shall be valued at both collaborating organizations.
- *Personal relationships* shall be built among individuals collaborating from each party, based on transparence, flexibility and mutual respect.
- *Suitable* formal and informal *communication mechanisms* shall be established.
- Acknowledged representatives shall be designated by both parties to act as stable liaisons between organizations.
- Collaborations shall be managed by *entrepreneurial* leaders with a global vision.

- Information produced during collaborations shall be treated *very respectfully*.
- A well-functioning collaboration shall be viewed as a *responsibility shared* by both parties.
- *Imagination and creativity* shall fuel collaborations to go forward.

Source: Exercise completed by several participants at ESADE's Executive Master in Public Administration.

Other Aspects Helping Collaboration Management

Mapping Each Sector's Function
It is necessary to clearly determine what public services will be managed by public administrations, which ones will be delivered by private organizations or associations, and which ones will be provided through collaborations. From the experiences in countries with a longer standing cross-sector collaboration record, we may draw several conclusions as to what services should be produced by administrations and private organizations, respectively (Table 3.5). As new social needs develop in the future, sector responsibilities should be reassessed to make the necessary adjustments.

Service Networks
As we have stated throughout this chapter, collaborations will work more effectively with the creation of local social service producing systems. In this scenario, local public sectors would be responsible for planning and coordinating the social service continuum required by the local population,

Table 3.5 Functions of nonprofit organizations and public administrations

Better produced by public agencies	Better produced by nonprofits
When it is important to prevent user discrimination	When customers cannot choose for themselves
When it is important for services to reach everyone	When services are associated with individual rights
When many resources are required for service supply	When services are labor-intensive
When there are no nonprofits traditionally providing this service	When services have been traditionally provided by nonprofits

Source: Elaborated by authors on the basis of Ferris and Graddy (1986), Gilbert (1985), and Osborne and Gaebler (1993).

while local private organizations would be committed to developing their service delivery capacity to suit local population needs, upon agreement with public agencies. We believe that, during economic crises, only public–private service networks may ensure social service supply in order to meet the requirements of entire populations.

Setting a Clearly defined Legal Framework

New laws should regulate and control social service outsourcing, providing for its transparence. System participants should know the ground rules and avoid at all costs the political strings that could be attached to a social service outsourcing system. Yet, excessive regulatory constraints should also be averted to prevent outsourcing from becoming ineffective.

Isolating Criticism from Management

To ensure the proper functioning of democratic systems, nonprofits must continue to criticize public and private institutions, actively advocating their customers'/users' rights. Public agencies should accept the advocacy role of nonprofits in society and in no way link outsourcing choices to "organizations' good behavior".

Developing Active Policies to Promote Market Making

Social service markets are not born overnight; efforts and resources must be dedicated to their emergence and development. In other words, if policies are not actively developed to promote nonprofits, there will be no guarantee whatsoever that users will be able to choose and prevent a few private organizations from holding newly created monopolies. Hence, public policies are required not only to set the necessary legal guidelines – as mentioned before – but also to foster nonprofit management improvements, to enhance their service quality and to contribute to boosting their productivity.

Social Entrepreneurs

Public and nonprofit practitioners are to play a new role in the system: they need to become social entrepreneurs. It will be their responsibility to drive the creation, development and continuous transformation of the social networks described in this passage.

Bogotá's City Hall

Colombia has also had its share of experience with political outsiders. It happened at the 1994 legislative elections. The new Constitution of 1991 had opened up elections for independent candidates, and a host of new candidates ran for governor and mayor, including churchmen, scholars, artists, men from the media, businessmen, and community leaders – a myriad of options for citizens to choose from. The list included a former dean of Colombia's National University, Antanas Mockus, a controversial, eccentric character who had been known to "lower his pants" to protest the government's neglect for higher education, running for mayor of Bogotá. Mockus filled the gap left by previous municipal administrations, characterized mainly by administrative inefficiency and an overall failure to solve the critical, urgent issues troubling the entire citizenship. Mockus championed the people's dissatisfaction with and disappointment in politics; he became the vehicle of criticism against the government, and he embodied the new hope of a non-politician getting into the game, supported by non-partisan citizens whose sole intention was to back an outsider to local politics. His candidacy was a magic trick, almost unthinkable in any Latin American country – much less in Colombian "macondian" politics, where everything is possible and magic tricks are customary. Antanas Mockus was driven to his victory by citizens from the informal sector: street vendors, cab drivers, students, free-lance workers, small storeowners and the unemployed. Although, of course, the administration of the former *Universidad Nacional* dean also elicited mixed opinions, many argue that he achieved effective results, particularly in the educational and civil fields. During his term in office, people in Bogotá started to wear their seatbelts; both drivers and pedestrians learnt what marked crossings were for, and bars closed at one in the morning. He is also credited with a transparent use of public resources and with effective efforts to set the city books in order.

Source: Red de investigadores latinoamericanos por la democracia y la autonomía de los pueblos: «Las convergencias democráticas en América Latina». (http://www.ufg.edu.sv).

Conclusions

The approach to public–private collaborations taken by many Western countries is not the best way to ensure that social and assistance public services are provided effectively and efficiently. The outsourcing method used to improve public service delivery – for example, in the case of street cleaning, waste collection, building maintenance, sports facilities and so on – is not suitable for the outsourcing of social aid services. We believe traditional business contracts cannot be applied to public–private collaborations.[4] Next, we intend to explain some of the factors involved in this problem.

Limitations of the traditional exchange system: time, learning and social dimensions

The traditional outsourcing system, based on transaction cost economics, features, at least, three significant restrictions that are usually ignored in topic debates – the time, learning and social dimensions (Berger *et al.*, 1993).

1. *Time dimension*. The time dimension will be easier to grasp by making a distinction between "transactions" and "relationships". *Transactions* are exchanges between one or more organizations at any given time. Each transaction is viewed as completely isolated from other exchanges between the parties. In a transaction, the future is treated as if it were present, and, thus, a contract with this perspective will reflect everything that will happen in the future. Instead, *relationships* are built for the long haul. From this outlook, exchanges may not be isolated from other exchanges between parties. Hence, contracts will have to adjust, necessarily, to the ongoing changes developing along the relationship (Macneil, 1974). In social and assistance services, the future is very hard to "pin down" in a contract. In our opinion, public–private collaborations for social and/or assistance services need to incorporate a time dimension, not only because future uncertainty is sizable, but also because, in cross-organization exchanges, relationships, far from being fixed, unravel and change over time.

2. *Learning dimension*. This dimension stems from the previous one. If we introduce a time dimension, relationship value does not rely exclusively on satisfying current contract demands, but on developing the required skills to understand and respond to new needs. This incorporates a new element in public–private collaborations. Organizations wishing to collaborate with public administrations will have to be scrutinized not only in their present structure, but also in their future potential and learning abilities.

3. *Social dimension*. Usually, collaborations are approached from a very individualistic outlook. They are construed as specific relationships between two organizations – in this case, a public and a private organization. Thus, organizations pursue their "own interest" to survive, and in collaborations, this will be the principle – conscious or otherwise – guiding their actions. Focusing on our "own interest", we fail to acknowledge the influence of social environments and, specifically, the relevance of a "charitable interest". Charitable motivations stem from a set of social norms people abide by because they feel "it is the right thing to do". Theoretically, a public–private relationship based on social norms rather than on individual interests seems more appealing. Therefore, outsourcing mechanisms should intend to "produce" social norms leading to a more generous relationship between organizations.

Toward a New Public–private Collaboration Model

If we incorporate the three dimensions described above, we can outline a new public–private collaboration model. Three objectives will guide this model:

1. In the production of a new social or assistance service through a public–private collaboration, the most important concern should be to ensure its *continuity*, as well as that of the entire complementary social service network. A private organization offering any given service outsourced by a public administration may, at the same time, offer, on its own or in combination with other public and private agencies, other additional services. Certainly, it will thus contribute to build a *social network*. "Severing" a section of that network may bring about terrible consequences for a group of users and organizations. Viewing social service outsourcing as a purely economic transaction reveals the short-sightedness of many public managers, often concerned by short-term budget cuts, who do not care much about the social system's long-term continuity.

2. Social service production through public–private collaborations constitutes an *ongoing learning process*. A salient characteristic in these relationships is that both parties learn during this process. Two-way knowledge exchanges take place, and both parties show an interest to improve the purpose of their relationship — in this case, a social and/or assistance service. Considering public–private collaborations as a process in which one of the parties controls operations while the other undertakes them does not allow for any knowledge development. For instance, if a private organization produces a service solely driven by monetary interest and its contract is dropped, it will try to take its experience with it, so that the new private organization hired to substitute for it will find it hard to operate. In a process of this kind, nobody learns anything.

3. Social service production should be construed not as a choice between public and private entities, but as a service to the entire community – not as the individual interest of each organization, but as a charitable interest. Quality social service production must be viewed as the interest of society at large. We should all want to offer a better education for our youngsters and good care for our elderly. Both public and private organizations acting in social and assistance services need to be driven by solidarity and not exclusively by their desire to survive as such. At this point, we must distinguish between two possible ways to interpret public–private collaborations. However, before we explain these different views, it should be noted that the instrument used to materialize an agreement between public and private organizations – the contract itself – is not questioned here. We do believe public–private relationships concerning social services ought to be documented by contracts. Still, we think it necessary for public and private practitioners to use a different approach to social service outsourcing development and management than the one used for other public and private services.

We shall use the term *competition model* to refer to the traditional view of public–private collaborations, whereas the term *collaboration model* will be used to designate the view of these relationships promoted by this book. This is an adaptation of Kettner and Martin's (1987) market association model. These two models are herein defined as follows:

1. *Competition model.* The relationship between the public and private sectors is based, essentially, on the outsourcing of certain standardized services. Suppliers periodically bid for these services, and their most relevant goal is to ensure contract renewal.
2. *Collaboration model.* The relationship between the public and private sectors is based, essentially, on a joint exploration of overall system needs (social dimension) and the shared belief that the most important goal is to improve and develop the system to provide quality services (learning dimension) for users over a lengthy period of time (time dimension).

CHAPTER 4

Collaborations Among Nonprofits: An Immediate Challenge

Introduction

The nonprofit sector, which is extremely diverse and plural, includes a large number of organizations of different sizes, cultures, origins and resources offering often similar services in very different areas, and features social awareness and relationships with administrations as key operating elements, should also focus on developing coordination links among its members.

This notion, at least theoretically recognized by most organizations, seldom translates, however, into collaboration practices, as may be drawn from the results of the few studies undertaken so far. Experts agree that the sector is not only extremely numerous, diversified, multi-shaped and plural but also fragmented and scattered.

The Phenomenon of Civil Society Organizations' Multiplication

A multi-shaped and plural third sector does not amount, in itself, to a negative factor. The dynamism featured by the sector and its leaders may be seen as a thermometer measuring both modern society's freedom and commitment. In addition, as pointed out by Turull and Negre (2002), people's identification with or sensibility toward specific social issues has greatly contributed to creating the large array of existing organizations. The nonprofit sector has consolidated from the bottom up – not the other way around – in a process that has determined its focus and geographic "capillarity", as well as its highly specialized nature. These characteristics may only thrive with proximity and commitment. Indeed, there is virtually no social need that has not given way to a new organization or a new program launched by an existing organization. In addition, nonprofit initiatives are rather swift in their execution, as opposed to public administrations, which usually due to their inherent bureaucracy, are slower in their innovating responses.

These features – flexibility, agility, proximity and social commitment – turn the nonprofit sector into a sound option in an environment shaped by deep social changes and transitions. As we have mentioned in our introductory chapter, Ullman (1998), for instance, believes that recent, international nonprofit proliferation is closely related to the so-called social State's double crisis: a fiscal crisis, because the State does not have enough resources to respond to all needs, and a capacity crisis, since, in general terms, the State is unable to honor its standing commitments to modern societies. The reasons underlying this capacity crisis are many. As suggested by Hood and Schuppert (1988), the increasing diversity of modern societies and the growing political relevance of minorities have become common characteristics, just as public service increase and diversification, rising service quality concerns and populations' ability to organize themselves aside from the State, as well as the increasing distrust of the public opinion in the public administration.

In short, as Ullman says, this double crisis translates into a policy of increasing responsibilities delegated by the State to private organizations, companies and, mostly, nonprofits – more efficient and effective for the delivery of specific social and welfare services. This assignment implies, therefore, overriding the charity culture to conceive nonprofit organizations as true social agents.

Finally, the message to convey here is that there is no ideal number of organizations for each intervention area, nor a maximum quota of nonprofits that should not be exceeded. That would actually undermine the very principles that serve as a basis for the third-sector self-regulation: freedom of association and social commitment. However, it is both true and disturbing that more and more organizations are "acting on their own" and there is no collaboration spirit to bind nonprofits operating in a single area.

Nonprofit Organizations' Environment

Negative Environmental Forces and Resistance to Collaboration

Why is collaboration still an exception rather than the rule, especially in its more advanced formats? Why do these sector organizations still mistrust each other? Understanding the key factors underlying this collaboration absence – almost systematic for some – is instrumental to minimizing their impact and fostering a collaboration culture.

Next, we summarize some of the factors that explain the low levels of systematic collaboration and coordination among third-sector organizations.

Competition for resources and users. The new institutional, operating and financial environment resulting from public policies that empower private organizations drives nonprofits and/or companies to compete for resources – mainly, service contracts – and service users. This strong competition effectively isolates organizations, zealously safeguarding their information and averting joint ventures with other nonprofits viewed as threats. Joint work between organizations is widely misrepresented, since it could actually help bring more resources onto the third sector.

Effort dissemination. This phenomenon is often found in second-tier structures, which have grown in number extensively over recent years to pursue a geographic, sector and institutional rationale. Often enough, coordinating agencies and federations of various local and domestic levels are found to have overlapping, uncoordinated tasks. In addition to jeopardizing their specific interventions, this situation hinders potential partnerships among organizations that, confused by the diversity and multiplicity of coordination efforts, are reluctant to allocate resources to these venues.

Time restraints. In any organization, the pressures and haste of daily operations obstruct strategic thinking – the basis for clearly defined missions and visions shared by the entire management team. Without clearly defined missions and visions, organizations find it very hard to converse with other organizations, since their respective identities would be at jeopardy.

Lack of resources. As we shall discuss later in this chapter, any collaboration process requires management, which also implies allocating resources, either material, financial or personal. As a result, collaborations may often be easier for large organizations having enough resources to spare.

Personalized organizations. Collaboration demands a listening disposition, a good dose of humbleness and a critical spirit, as well as some curiosity for others and the will to tolerate differences – all of these characteristics are hardly found in highly personalized organizations.

Change-averse organizational cultures. Organizations are often reluctant to collaborations when they resist change and new ideas. These organizations, lacking in creativity and clear visions, usually stick to obsolete rules and regulations and fear a loss of authority.

Negative previous experiences. Endless meetings without any specific objectives in sight; an inability to manage information flows; unmet expectations; no tangible, short-term results; troublesome communications; "hostage" feelings when "everything has already been decided" – these are all previous experiences that, once organizations have faced them in failed collaborations, act as deterrents for any new collaboration initiatives that may surface in the future.

Positive Environmental Forces Fostering Greater Collaboration among Third-sector Organizations

Indeed, it is difficult to change the fragmented third-sector status quo with easy statements like "collaboration is good". Neither is it possible to impose collaboration practices from outside the nonprofit sector, where individual values are essential and organizations relentlessly preserve their own identities that stem from specific values. However, the fact remains that the environment has evolved greatly in recent years, and several trends are currently promoting further collaboration among nonprofit organizations. As Turull and Negre (2002) point out, the present setting, marked by deep and rapid changes, should not go unnoticed by nonprofits. On the contrary, volunteer organizations face a great opportunity to consolidate and strengthen if they act strategically and adjust to new needs and demands.

Next, we discuss some of the trends and phenomena fostering collaboration among nonprofits.

The emergence of complex issues requires diversified, cross-sector and multi-disciplinary approaches, for their solutions far exceed the capacity of any one organization. In recent years, for example, a host of new forums, platforms and campaigns have been launched by many nonprofit organizations to raise awareness on arms trade, external debt, immigration or increasing globalization.

The growth in demand for accountability, efficient resource utilization and rationalization in service supply that some funding agencies are already expecting – though in some sectors more than others. For instance, development cooperation is one of the areas in which organizations are starting to carry out systematic audits and ex-post assessments to measure intervention results and impacts.

Users' and beneficiaries' desire for greater coordination among the organizations they work with. Although a broader offer benefits citizens, for they can choose who to turn to for assistance, excessive offer fragmentation may also confuse nonprofit users, beneficiaries and the general public.

Public administrations' acknowledgement of third-sector organizations as political agents in their own right, whom they need to communicate with, and their necessity to identify a few legitimate representatives of the third sector to interact with. The increase in publications of civic-social sector studies shows not only public administrations' rising interest in the nonprofit sector, but also the departure from the charity culture of the past and a new perception of nonprofits as legitimate, socially responsible agents.

The development of new technologies provides an array of information and communication breakthroughs – in velocity, cost reductions and so on – that bear a significant impact on organizational structures – for instance, offering a real option for decentralized work, ensuring remote coordination and so on.

Collaboration as an End: Why is Collaboration Necessary?

Against this new backdrop that signals the transition to an increasingly relational society, where the public realm no longer pertains exclusively to the State and becomes a domain shared by State and society in its multiple forms, the nonprofit sector emerges as one of society's especially suited organizational forms to warrant and streamline social involvement. Nonprofit organizations enable the exercise of mature democracy as opposed to low-intensity democracy – that is, "the mediation and intermediation between individuals and the State, social mobilization and the defense of individual and collective rights, the links to territories and to identity and proximity elements, the solution to collective problems and the delivery of social services" (FCE, 2000).

However, we should not fool ourselves. Only a plural yet cohesive and coordinated third sector will be able to step into its role in the new social model currently unfolding. Thus, the third sector's characteristic fragmentation and dispersion constitute true hindrances for nonprofits desiring to contribute their share to building a new model for society.

Limitations to the "Small is Beautiful" Slogan

In international development, the "small is beautiful" dictum, which had shaped many of the most innovating NGO experiences throughout the 1980s, contributed to exposing the severe shortcomings in the approach of bilateral and multilateral agencies, focusing on large infrastructure and turnaround projects – most of which grossly overlooked the human and social factor in developing countries. Yet, NGOs' "close-to-communities" approach has also shown its own weaknesses, especially its lack of coordination and its fragmented efforts. Oftentimes, these weaknesses simply reflect the civil society that has built and joined these organizations: a rich civil society that responds to social changes but features great subjectivity. Twenty years later, amidst the onslaught of globalization, NGO coordination is still a pressing, unresolved matter.

From an institutional viewpoint, fragmentation, translated into the image of a disorganized and uncoordinated sector, brings about credibility and legitimacy issues for society at large, and for public administrations and private sector agents specifically. On the one hand, dispersion makes it hard for others to identify valid sector representatives that are able to advocate the sector's collective interests. On the other hand, despite its increasing numbers and virtues, the sector is not perceived as such by society; rather, it is still regarded as an isolated phenomenon. Finally, the lack of coordination hinders the building of relationships with the other two sectors – public and private for-profit, as we have already discussed in previous chapters.

From an operational viewpoint, fragmentation and dispersion often imply effort redundancy – in economic terms: duplicating undifferentiated offers – and incoherent actions. For instance, in the field of humanitarian relief in conflict-stricken areas, uncoordinated and even contradictory approaches by several agents must often be resolved to prevent the impact of these interventions being rendered useless while the proliferation of organizations turns into a "circus" of sorts.

From the managerial viewpoint, effectiveness and efficiency criteria are also relevant and should also be factored in nonprofit interventions. While we advocate for the sector's plurality and appreciate the value of the links and proximity of its organizations, the fact that many associations act on their own – as we stated in the previous section – is indeed worrisome. Perhaps, we should get used to the idea that when a new program or project is suggested in an organization, the first questions are not how many volunteers are needed, what is the required budget or how to communicate the initiative to the general public. Instead, we should wonder whether there is another organization offering the same service or undertaking the same action, whether the program or project could be better served through a collaboration with another organization to ensure its effectiveness and quality, whether the impact of this initiative could be enhanced through joint activities with other organizations, whether an organization's action could be exploited to inform the public about other organizations or other similar programs delivered by other nonprofits. In a nutshell, organizations should consider whether they are more effective and efficient in their fields by working on their own or in collaboration with other nonprofits.

Finally, and especially for smaller organizations feeling the pressure of the new managerial demands resulting from an increasingly competitive environment, collaboration is a must for survival. As we shall discuss later in this chapter, second-tier organizations may play a crucial role by providing management services to smaller organizations lacking the necessary resources to afford these functions.

Collaboration Benefits

To conclude, though with no claim for thoroughness, here are some of the benefits that may be accrued through sound collaborations among third-sector organizations.

From the point of view of an organization

- Collaborations contribute to enhance organizational *efficiency* and resource optimization through phenomena such as economies of scale, experience sharing and so on.
- Collaborations may *increase the impact*, reach and coherence of sector interventions, enabling organizations to address more complex issues requiring multi-disciplinary and cross-sectional approaches.
- Collaborations may help organizations to adjust to the environment by providing opportunities for mutual *learning* and experience exchanges.
- Collaborations boost nonprofits' strength and *negotiating leverage* for future transactions.
- Collaborations among nonprofits may turn out to be an additional appeal for *collaboration agreements with business companies and/or public administrations*.

From the point of view of the sector

- "The whole is more than the sum of its parts", on account of intervention complementariness and created *synergies*.
- Collaborations allow for the development of social *self-control and self-regulating* mechanisms, designed by sector organizations.

- Collaborations contribute to developing agents' *co-responsibility* culture and cooperative skills – such as openness, trust and transparence.
- Collaborations help the sector consolidate and improve its *social positioning*. A plural, yet coordinated sector is more legitimate and trustworthy for society and other agents – public administrations and business companies – as well.

Some of these benefits have been sharply clarified by actual experiences, such as the *campaign for transparence and weapon control* ("Farewell to Arms") launched, in the Spain case, jointly by Amnesty International, Greenpeace, Intermón Oxfam and Médecins Sans Frontières (MSF) a few years ago. The most salient conclusions drawn from this collaboration venture are summarized below (Vernis, 1998a).

"Farewell to Arms" Campaign in Spain

The following are five campaign advantages that may be applicable to many collaborations among nonprofits:

- *Consensus message.* Consensual actions among several organizations convey a message of "teamwork", of joining efforts.
- *Internal learning.* Collaborations provide an excellent opportunity to learn new ways of working and operating from other organizations. Organizations may exploit collaborations as means to acquire new knowledge.
- *Enhanced impact.* When organizations work together, their actions become stronger, louder and more reliable. For instance, a project will reach farther if several organizations collaborate to develop it than if an organization implements it single-handedly.
- *Ideological enrichment.* Participating in a project with other organizations allows for the ideological enrichment of the people involved, who find themselves exposed to different ways of thinking. In short, collaborations constitute a unique opportunity for new ideas to permeate organizations and, in turn, for organizations to "export" their own ideas to others.
- *Mutual trust.* Collaborations build mutual trust among nonprofits, which will surely consult each other and suggest new joint ventures in the future.

The Collaboration Continuum

There are no rigid categories to classify collaboration models for nonprofits. Quite the contrary, collaboration formats are multiple as a result of the myriad scenarios, motivations and goals driving nonprofit organizations to approach one another. In general, nonprofits tend to come together in collaborations that may be categorized according to the following criteria:

- *Time span*. Collaborations may be specific and temporary – for a single program or project – or permanent – to create new joint work venues, such as forums, platforms and so on.
- *Collaboration objectives*. Collaborations may be forged to foster communications, especially with other parties, to ensure sector legitimacy and message cohesion – for example, the work done by second-tier organizations and networks – or to develop a joint program, such as a specific campaign.
- *Operating field*. Collaborations may be service-oriented or geographically based, for example.
- *Commitment and resources demanded*. Collaborations have endless possibilities, going from mere information dissemination or virtual network involvement to the need to adjust operations, share resources and strengthen capabilities – not only to benefit all members but also to attain a common goal.

In addition, collaborations are not static: they evolve in time, as actors get to know each other and build trust among themselves.

As we suggested in Chapter 2, where we discussed collaborations between the third and business sectors, it may be useful to view collaborations among nonprofits as a continuum (adapted from Austin, 2001b), featuring, in one extreme, collaborations that may be defined as *anecdotic*, characterized by minimum commitment and maintained autonomy for all parties and, in the other extreme, *integrated* collaborations, characterized by a stable relationship, high commitment and autonomy/sovereignty loss by all parties to serve the whole (Figure 4.1). Between these two extremes, we find the collaborations we have defined as *operative* and *strategic*.

As was the case in cross-sector collaborations between business companies and nonprofits, collaborations among social organizations do not necessarily go through all four stages. In fact, unfortunately, only a few ever reach the strategic phase, and fewer still manage to build integrated partnerships. Alliances among organizations may evolve through the collaboration continuum in an unplanned fashion. Yet, despite any pre-conceptions, organizations need not have any affinity or common traits to embark on collaborations. When both parties share the disposition to collaborate, organizations always find a common ground to build their partnership.

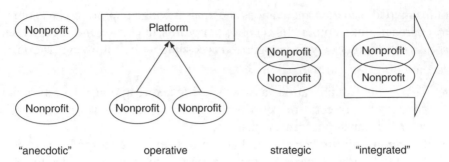

Figure 4.1   Collaboration levels. *Source*: Elaborated by authors, based on Austin, 2000

Phase	Anecdotic	Operative	Strategic	Integrated
Commitment	Low			High
Mission relevance	Low			High
Resources	Few			Many
Action objectives	Specific			Broad
Interaction rhythm	Low			High
Management complexity	Low			High
Strategic value	Low			High
Relationship stability	Low			High

Figure 4.2   Collaboration phases. *Source*: Adapted from Austin, 2001b

Collaboration Models

By no means attempting to be thorough, we shall next analyze some of the most usual collaboration formats preferred by nonprofit organizations (own categorization based on Vernis, 1998a, and Arsenault, 1998).

Networks

Networking constitutes one of the most flexible collaboration forms on account of its low formalization. This format, profusely developed in recent years as a result of new technologies that have enabled enhanced, low-cost information flows, calls for, in general terms and as compared to other more formal collaboration formats, low levels of mutual trust and commitment among member organizations. In addition, networks allow member organizations to retain their autonomy.

Generally, networks feature the following traits (Itriago and Itriago, 2000):

- There is no vertical hierarchy among members. Network structures are usually flat and very flexible, thus allowing for, in some cases, temporary partnering.
- Networks may integrate structures of different nature and size. For example, Independent Sector, devoted to promoting philanthropy, volunteer work, nonprofit initiatives and social aid, gathers over 700 US organizations – foundations, nonprofits and companies – committed to citizenship and third-sector development.
- Usually, networks have their own objectives and specific activities, rather than pursuing the collective goals of their members. For instance, a network objective could be to provide a political forum for the grassroots organizations in a given community.
- Networks are based on an interactivity principle.
- In general, this formula is used for information and experience exchanges intended to benefit network members.

Cameroon's National Population Network

By Mauricio Floridi, sociologist and international consultant specializing in local development dynamics and institutional strengthening.

Created in 1997 in Yaoundé, Cameroon's political capital, by a group of grassroots organizations' leaders, this network, fueled by a small local association (ASSOAL), operates today in 15 Cameroon cities, gathering over 1500 organizations and involving in excess of 70,000 people. Most of its member organizations belong to the so-called "informal sector", since they have no formal by-laws or definite legal status, but they are very active in what may be referred to as community governance. The activities undertaken by these organizations cover hygiene issues, such as waste disposal, community awareness on water utilization, etc.; the fight against crime, collaborating with law enforcement forces to curb violence, maintenance of public lighting, etc.; social and collective services,

Continued

such as the creation of daycare centers for working women's children, local school and library upkeep, etc., and employment promotion, among others.

On the basis of the activities undertaken by community organizations, Cameroon's Population Network, despite its lack of legal inception, has become a legitimate counterpart for public agencies, city administrations and cooperation agencies when it comes to discussing and negotiating urban development processes in each town.

Organizations do not need to register in order to join the Network; they are just required to adhere to the *Network's Values Charter*. This is a true declaration of principles that revolve around the idea that citizens cannot idly wait for State officials to take action; rather, they must lead their cities to development and change through their own ideas, resources and actions.

Thus, each of the organizations involved, which preserve their identity and autonomy, is a part of a much larger movement that concerns the whole nation and, also, crosses its borders with initiatives such as the Inter African Population Forum (Dakar, 1998 and Harare, 2000).

Second-tier Structures

Second-tier structures, primarily federations, are created by groups of organizations sharing common goals to provide an umbrella coverage and to ensure their access to information or to other agents – particularly public administrations – by coordinating and voicing common interests.

These structures may be geographically based or field-oriented. Territorial structures emerge to coordinate the actions of several organizations operating in a single location. Sector structures surface to coordinate the operations of several organizations that share target segments or fields and have similar goals.

The Example of the Federations of Agricultural Organizations in Some African countries

In some African nations, territorial federations of farmers' organizations have grown and spread enormously since the 1980s. Fully self-funded through members' contributions, these structures have enabled the introduction of all kinds of innovations not only in agriculture but also in the local economic and social conditions, which would have been impossible to promote in members' communities. Through the training of farmers in more suitable planting techniques for each environment, the creation of loan cooperatives to support micro-ventures, or the organization of product distribution, storage and collective price negotiation, as well as the introduction of literacy classes and small community infrastructures, federations have become the true drivers for local development in several African regions.

The incentives found by nonprofits to engage in these structures include the following: keeping in touch with other organizations, exchanging experiences and insights, enhancing their technical capabilities, securing feasibility, influence and legitimacy, and lobbying for public funding.

Belonging to second-tier structures affects organizations' operations on several levels. On the one hand, it implies an economic cost that organizations must bear – membership fees, traveling expenses for representatives to attend structure governance meetings and so on. On the other hand, it implies that organizations are interested in developing functions that go beyond the boundaries of their specific and individual interventions and entrust these functions to entities that represent many organizations at a time. Thus, joining a second-tier structure denotes a certain loss of autonomy for member organizations, since they decide to adhere to the "politics" and "strategies" set by second-tier structures.

Some of these structures, with clearly defined missions, have attained significant accomplishments for their member organizations. Still, as we mentioned when we discussed environmental, positive and negative forces affecting collaborations in the nonprofit world, effort fragmentation is a common occurrence in second-tier structures, which have proliferated widely in recent years. Often enough, several second-tier structures operate in the same field, with vaguely defined missions and overlapping, uncoordinated roles. On occasion, they even compete for resources with their own member organizations. One of the tasks of these structures is to offer administrative and managerial services to their members. This scheme, which we shall discuss in more detail in the following section, may account for an opportunity to provide real content to second-tier structures.

Relationships with Other Organizations

Collaborations to undertake specific projects or organize joint events, to outsource services, to participate in consulting bodies, to advice on projects, to lend facilities or donations and so on are other forms used by nonprofits to relate to each other. In these cases, the global effect amounts to saving resources through the creation of economies of scale, or a greater reach for operations.

Particularly in its most advanced forms, which exceed the relationship frequently built between funding agencies and service providers, this type of collaborations is seldom found. Perhaps, this is because, in addition to an exchange of information between collaborating organizations, it demands high commitment and some involvement from each party – which translates into the definition of common objectives and activity coordination. In some cases, depending on the collaboration type, this scheme may also imply sharing resources and responsibilities, not only to benefit the parties engaged, but also for a specific purpose. Finally, as we shall discuss later when we delve into subtypes, this kind of collaboration may entail a partial or total loss of autonomy and identity for the organizations involved.

As we stated before, the possibilities for nonprofits to relate to other organizations are very diverse. Next, we analyze some formats that have become more customary.

Undertaking joint campaigns

A specific, worth-mentioning case is the collaboration to advocate for certain rights, to protest against injustices or to raise awareness on some issues. There are numerous examples of this collaboration type, characterized by the fact that participating organizations keep their autonomy despite their coordination to develop a joint project. In general, these collaborations also feature a definite time frame. For example, joint fund-raising campaigns are quite frequent. Still, initially planned time frames may be extended for campaigns, other than specific fund-raisers, that eventually turn into rather permanent platforms and forums. A current example is the international 2000 Jubilee movement for external debt condonation, active in over fifty nations. This collaboration has become a network – of the kind we described above.

Undertaking joint programs

This collaboration type involves moving forward along the continuum we referred to in the previous section. Usually, the organizations that decide to work together in a program partner for the medium term. As a result, their autonomy – even their decision-making sovereignty – is left temporarily aside for a common effort. Such is the case, for example, of development cooperation ventures, in which highly specialized organizations from various fields, such as health, education, social mobilization and so on, decide to come together to address a complex issue requiring a multi-disciplinary approach – for instance, the development of a community in a developing country. Each organization contributes its experience to benefit the partnership, and, through the synergies created, the intended intervention results in a whole that exceeds the sum of its parts.

Management service organizations

These collaborations are built to create a new entity that will offer management and administrative services to other organizations in order to boost effectiveness and efficiency in one or several management functions.

There are two primary models. The first model involves an organization that has sufficient administrative capability and decides to share it with others. Such is usually the case of large organizations that are able to offer managerial services to smaller organizations, which, on account of their size and limited resources, could not insure these services otherwise. Also, there are foundations that specialize in training nonprofits or designing larger-scale support programs. The second model emerges when several organizations come together to create a new organization to provide administrative services to founding organizations. This is the model that would apply to the second-tier structures we referred to before.

Civil Society Organization Movements

These movements are built domestically or internationally, like Médecins Sans Frontières (MSF), Oxfam, Action Aid or CARE, and they include several organizations with equal goals and similar identities, primarily differentiated by their operations' location (Lindenberg and Dobel, 1999).[1] Depending on the structure, member organizations share not only their name and mission core, but also managerial guidelines and procedures.

Collaboration Management

Collaborations among nonprofit organizations take multiple forms – including, though not exclusively, the formats we have outlined before. Collaboration types mostly depend on the disposition and imagination of participating organizations.

Regardless of this diversity and in line with what we have discussed in the past two chapters, the point is that, to build collaborations with other sector organizations, nonprofits need to consider that any partnership process must fulfill several requirements in order to work. Indeed, collaboration may be defined as a process that requires management, to a greater or lesser extent, depending on the efforts demanded by the chosen format. For instance, a simple coalition should not necessarily be viewed as a collaboration. To work with other organizations, each collaborator (organization and actor) ought to understand the collaboration process and product.

Next, we summarize some of the key components involved in successful collaborations.

Information and Communications

- In spite of individual specificities, organizations engaged in a collaboration process must share a common *vision* and understanding of the collaboration type to be pursued and its implications. Collaborations should not go against the nature of the organizations involved.
- Collaborating organizations must *contribute ideas, experience and information*. Thus, transparence is a key component in successful collaborations. In addition, member organizations should be accountable for their actions to the other collaboration participants.
- Collaborations must be based on *fluent and ongoing communications* between partner organizations. It is also important for collaborating organizations to formulate a common language, acknowledged and understood by all parties.

Professionalism and Management Capability

- Collaborations need to be *managed; the necessary people and means must be assigned to set collaboration objectives* and to monitor and assess them. It is also important for the collaboration to be formalized in some way, either through the creation of a new organization, the use of an intermediary organization or a signed agreement or declaration. One of the purposes of formal inception is to assign responsibilities and tasks so that "accountability" is based on actual premises.
- *Individual and collective accountability systems* should be established, adding to the necessary mechanisms for periodical evaluations and collaboration progress measurements.

Mutual Support and Trust

- Organizations must get to know each other, building mutual *trust* among them. Trust is based on both hard – power, money, law – and soft factors – culture, organizations' expectations. It should be noted, also, that collaboration format and involvement methods used to engage all stakeholders will bear an impact on the trust built among organizations.

- Each member organization should try *to maximize its strengths* to benefit all other partners. A key factor to collaboration success lies in identifying leaders on the basis of individual organization's strengths.

Motivation

- Organizations engaging in collaborations must be highly *motivated* and convinced that these partnerships will be useful and beneficial. Collaboration processes, especially the most advanced formats, imply a negotiation among member organizations regarding mutually compatible objectives and strategies to accomplish them. It is important that each organization feels that they are all working to reach a "win-all" agreement – that is an agreement that ensures that collaboration benefits override the "cost" associated with efforts made.
- Collaborations should focus on clear goals, and organizations must be committed to their achievement.
- The *territorial dimension* of collaborations should be carefully regarded, since, as is the case for each organization (proximity factor), it turns out to be instrumental to most association processes. In short, as we have already pointed out, collaborations should not go against member organization features – and, among them, territorial aspects.

Next, we include a guide (Table 4.1) to guide and manage collaboration processes on the basis of the requirements we have just outlined.

Table 4.1 Suggested guidelines to initiate and manage collaboration processes[2]

A guide to initiate and manage collaboration processes	
Phase 1: Specifying individual motivations for collaborations	
Organizations	What is the rationale fueling a collaboration process? What benefits are expected? Is the organization prepared to engage in a process of this kind? What resources are available and how many are to be assigned to the collaboration?
Actors	Which other organizations are involved in the process? What are their missions? And their expectations? What do we expect from them? Do the parties involved trust each other? To what extent?

Table 4.1 (Continued)	
Phase 2: Defining the issue to be addressed	
Process principles	How do we view the process? What about the other actors involved?
	List collaboration objectives (global and specific goals). Are these objectives shared by all actors involved? Are they compatible with our mission? Will these objectives add to the accomplishment of our organization's goals?
	Do we know of other experiences bearing similar objectives? How did they turn out?
	What are the risks involved in this collaboration?
Phase 3: Specifying parties' contributions and roles	
Resources	In each organization, who will be directly involved in the collaboration?
	Is special training required?
	Is there a suitable incentive system? Which one?
	What resources will be contributed by each organization? How will financial resources be obtained?
	Is there a global financial plan for the entire collaboration and a clearly defined strategy featuring specific responsibilities for each party?
Phase 4: Specifying collaboration and decision-making processes	
Process materialization	How will "the agreement" be materialized?
	What systems should be established for collaboration management and supervision?
	What are the implications of these systems for our organization?
	How will collaboration results be measured?
Leadership	Who leads this process? Do all actors agree?
	Is this leadership enough? How could it be enhanced?
Decision-making and communications	Who will make the necessary decisions? How relevant and binding are decisions?
	Definition of responsibility levels.
	How will we ensure unequivocal leadership and maintain diversity at the same time?
	What information and communication mechanisms will be used internally?
	To what extent will the process be communicated externally? Is there a communication plan?
Phase 5: Joint definition of collaboration success, failure and conclusion	
Conflicts	What barriers and conflicts hinder or could eventually hinder process evolution?
	How could these obstacles be mitigated or offset?
Conclusion	How should the experience be assessed?
	How could we exploit it?

Conclusions: Some Tips to Improve Collaborations Among Nonprofits

What can organizations do to break away from the sector fragmentation and dispersion we have referred to at the beginning of this chapter? How could we boost our domestic collaboration culture among nonprofits and foundations?

To conclude, we shall explore the factors that may contribute to enhancing collaborations among nonprofit organizations.

A shift in sector collaboration culture. For the relational structure to change, first nonprofits should experience a deep mindset transformation to perceive collaboration not only as an opportunity but also as a need in the current transition toward a relational society. In addition to viewing collaboration as a fund-raising instrument, organizations should regard it as one of the strategies pursued to reach their goals. Nonprofits must come to view each other as complementary to ensure that the coordinated sum of their efforts leads to improved sector results.

Creation of collaboration-specific internal areas. Organizations need to develop specific areas, featuring suitable technological means, for relational and communication work with other nonprofits acting in similar fields and/or territories. Coordination with other organizations should become an additional function within each organization, entrusted to a specific individual or group of individuals in pursuit of explicit objectives.

Training. Although "disposition" is a core ingredient in organizations' operations and there should be an overall mindset change across the third sector, organizations must rely on specific instruments to manage collaborations. These instruments are to be acquired. To this end, training plays an essential role in collaboration promotion, not only to ensure the necessary organizational learning associated with collaboration management and relational work instruments, but also for the sector to convey its global vision outside the specific sphere of each organization. Additionally, training program formulation also affords an opportunity to work with other organizations, designing contents based on common interests, adding and exploiting available resources.

Public sector actions. Public administrations should foster nonprofit collaborations, both in their role as funding agencies – prioritizing joint initiatives and funding collaboration processes – and providing specific venues to promote sector exchanges. The European Commission's special funding for decentralized cooperation (http://europa.eu.int/comm/europeaid/

index_en.htm) adequately illustrates a policy of resource allocation to collaboration initiatives in developing countries.

Second-tier structure consolidation. Second-tier structures will play an increasingly relevant role in a scenario requiring legitimate third-sector representatives. To take up this role, second-tier structures need to consolidate, rationalizing their interventions and strategically redesigning their operations. Also, these structures will demand greater commitment from their members and other agents – such as public administrations, which should pay more attention to sector needs and provide the necessary resources to support consolidation processes, rather than simply delegating the responsibility for some social and welfare services to nonprofits. Another key consolidating factor for second-tier structures lies in their transformation to become effective management service organizations, supporting smaller organizations that need assistance to face the increasingly demanding and competitive environment of the present.

PART II

Competencies Required for Third-Sector Capacity Building

In the first part of this book, we discussed collaboration as an essential instrument for capacity building. In the second part, we shall focus on the three primary competences required, in our opinion, for nonprofit organizations to face collaboration challenges. These three competences are governance, accountability and human resources. We believe that lest these competences are strengthened, everything we have outlined in the first part of our book is doomed to fail.[1]

First, if boards are not reinforced, strategic partnerships cannot be built with business companies, public administrations and/or other nonprofits. Second, if third-sector organizations fail to become more transparent, if their operations are not accounted for in a clear fashion, nonprofits will not build the necessary trust for other actors to be willing to collaborate with them. Lastly, the competencies exhibited by the people who work and collaborate with nonprofits will ultimately lead and drive collaboration processes.

As we discussed in the first chapter, we believe capacity building amounts to a third stage in nonprofit organizations' management, and these competencies will eventually lead to the consolidation of the sector.

The model we have presented includes, at its center, the specific third-sector values, so that all nonprofit management improvements revolve around them (Figure PII.1). In other words, the location of these values indicates that nonprofits' effectiveness and efficiency enhancements cannot focus solely on improving economic results, but also on the sector's intrinsic values. Thus, for instance, the application of a coherent human resources policy should be an aspiration of all nonprofits, since the respect for individuals and their jobs must be a core value for the third sector. The same goes for communications or fund-raising policies. Over the

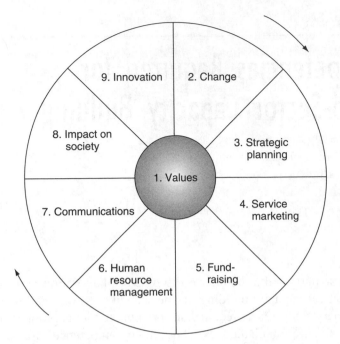

Figure PII.I   Nonprofit management improvement model. (*Source*: Vernis *et al.*, 1998)

years, we have explained this model in different forums and proven its usefulness by studying the way in which so many nonprofits operate.

After considering values as the differentiating factor for nonprofits, we should ask ourselves if *the management culture is the most applicable to nonprofit organizations and foundations*. Indeed, we have already pointed out that management culture advocates claim that this culture, based on effectiveness and efficiency, should also be applied to volunteer organizations for two reasons. First, because of the increased responsibilities borne by nonprofits, which demand specific skills and specialization from the people working in the sector. This specialization, we argued, may not be ensured solely by means of volunteers, and, thus, management professionalization also becomes necessary. The second reason lies in the fact that the number of volunteers committing to nonprofits is increasing. Both factors effectively increase the need for a more effective and efficient management of nonprofit organizations and foundations.

Furthermore, we have also explained that the people who oppose the application of the management culture to nonprofits offer two arguments that should be taken into account. First, volunteer work is necessarily associated with the notion of freedom and does not operate in structures based in a line of command. Second, an excessive formalization of nonprofits may ostracize people or groups who dislike or fear excessively formal or rigid operations.

We do support the application of the management culture to third-sector organizations, with the caveat that their specific values be preserved, for they provide its unique character.

We have chosen to position these core values on the center of our circular model because they should act as an axis to all organizational operations. Also, this circle illustrates our representation of nonprofit operations – ongoing change – and provides a launching pad to plunge into the managerial challenges faced by nonprofits. To the initial two concentric circles in the model, we now add a third circle, that features the competences nonprofits should possess in order to ensure their capacity building. The resulting construct is shown in Figure PII.2.

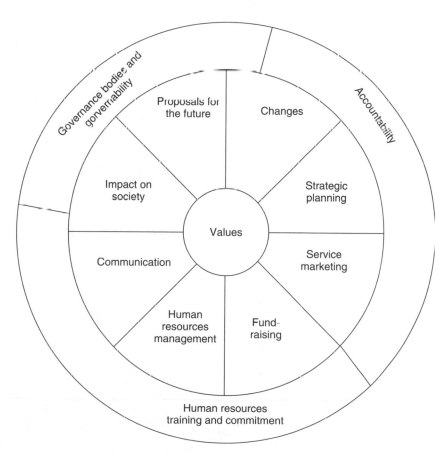

Figure PII.2   Nonprofits' capacity building

We have focused the second part of this book on three primary competences for capacity building. Although there are others, we have chosen these three – governance, accountability and human resources training and commitment – in order to, first, prevent our book from becoming far too long and, secondly, to indicate and reinforce the essential and instrumental nature of these competences. If we had to broaden our selection to include other primary competences that would drive nonprofits' capacity building, we would surely favor the use of new technologies, innovation and creativity, broad and committed social mobilization, political impact and awareness-raising potential. However, these competences truly deserve a book of their own.

CHAPTER 5

Accountability Elements in Nonprofits

Introduction

"NGOs are influential. Nevertheless, in the future, their lack of accountability and legitimacy will curtail – or, at least, restraint – their influence capabilities." Many of the people who collaborate with or work at nonprofit organizations will surely agree with this statement by University of Oxford Professor Alan M. Rugman (2001). Civil society organizations still need to prove to a significant share of western societies that they are not mere charitable institutions, service providers or anti-establishment activists.

If civil society organizations expect to exert a real influence, they must, now that they have come of age, rise to the challenge of becoming trustworthy for most of the nation's population. Hence, it is paramount for them to explain their operations rigorously, primarily to secure their legitimacy in society. Nonprofit organizations require – probably more than business companies and public administrations – large doses of trust, and trust must be built. This implies, first, *doing* – that is, ensuring all actions match organizational values and creating the necessary systems to guarantee these values are respected. Secondly, to build trust, nonprofits need to communicate their way of doing things with transparency and thoroughness.

Who Controls Nonprofits?

Civil society organizations make the headlines almost exclusively when there is a scandal. At the same time, the people who work at and collaborate with nonprofits often complain that society only shows its solidarity when catastrophes strike. We are well aware of the general reaction to the tsunami in Southeast Asia, the Mitch hurricane in Central America or the massive exodus out of Kosovo. We still remember, farther back, the humanitarian response to the war in Bosnia or the tragedy at the Great Lakes area. Natural and human disasters make the news, and the media vehemently cover them. However, the rest of the time, as we have pointed out in our introduction, the regular operations of most nonprofits in very many fields go largely unnoticed by the general public.

Thus, it should not come as a surprise that nonprofits are still widely unknown to a large segment of society. Questions regarding who controls nonprofits or whether the financial scandals portrayed by headlines are widespread in the sector or just isolated cases are becoming increasingly common in our society.

The answer to the first question should be rather simple – at least theoretically: nonprofit organizations' governance bodies are responsible for controlling their operations, since they are at the end of their responsibility chain. However, in practical terms, many problems often arise when it comes to overseeing nonprofits' operations. For example, all too often, nonprofits' board members are too busy to attend regular meetings or to devote any time to organizational follow-up. In addition, also quite frequently, these people are involved in more than a single board at the same time. We shall discuss nonprofit governance bodies in depth in the next chapter.

The answer to the second question is quite clear: few nonprofit organizations engage in practices that go against third-sector values. Regrettably, like in the other two – public and private for-profit – sectors, and despite the control mechanisms set in place by each organization and society as well, in some cases, the misguided practices of these organizations end up damaging the public image of the entire sector. It should be noted, though, that society's trust does not respond to any one specific organization. In fact, experience has proven that an ethical issue or corruption case in one or several sector organizations may affect – and usually does – all other organizations in the sector, whose credibility is also questioned by society.

Why Is It So Hard to Control Third-sector Organizations' Operations?

Since there is no clearly defined measurement for nonprofit organizations' results, the main difficulty lies in setting controls for third sector operations – unlike what happens in the other two sectors. As M. Edwards and D. Hulme (1996) state, "measuring the results of nonprofit organizations is a complicated matter". In private companies, controls are set on the basis of three mechanisms that are not available – theoretically, at least – in the nonprofit sector. These mechanisms are the following:

1. Business results are measured in terms of earnings and losses, with instruments such as profit and loss statements, balance sheets and so on.
2. Shareholders, who have invested in companies, control their operations.
3. Outside organizations, the *market rules*: the market is a highly competitive environment that drives companies and forces them to control each of their operations.

Similarly, public administrations are held accountable for their operations and have several control mechanisms. Ultimately, their operations are regulated by means of elections.[1]

Why Should Nonprofit Organizations be Held Accountable?

In other words, why is it important for volunteer organizations and foundations to rigorously account for their operations? The answer, as we anticipated in our introduction to this section, is simple: *to build trust*. Unless nonprofits rigorously and continuously feed society with truthful and transparent information on their operations, the trust society still puts in the sector will gradually dwindle.

Some people in the third-sector demand nonprofit autonomy and independence, claiming that autonomy does not require accounting for their operations to outsiders. Perhaps this claim could be upheld as long as nonprofit operations had no public impact and their funding came solely from private sources. However, very few western nonprofit organizations today can rightfully claim to be financially independent. Greenpeace is one of them and, yet, accountability is one of its guiding principles. Most third-sector organizations get their funding from individuals, public administrations and, to a lesser extent, business companies and other foundations. Therefore, we are talking about public money, and nonprofits must account for their use of that money. In addition, there are many organizations whose interventions have a social impact that goes beyond their specific field of action. Organizations need to account for their actions not only to their partners and immediate collaborates, but to society at large.

What Is Accountability and Why Is It So Important for Nonprofits?

Kearns (1996) makes a distinction between a very specific and a broader definition of the term *accountability*. The specific definition refers to legal guidelines regulating third-sector organizations. The broad definition, used in this chapter, promotes the notion of responding to society at large not only on legal aspects, but also on everything that relates to organizations' operations.

It should be noted that accountability engulfs far more than purely economic and financial matters. Thus, it does not suffice to submit organizations' financial statements and publish them on the Internet, or exposing the results of annual audits. Economic and financial transparency is necessary in organizations and is also part of the notion of accountability. However, this concept goes beyond publicity, since it entails reporting to all the people who have supported an organization, and to society at large, what has been done during a specific period of time.

Neither should we confuse accountability with nonprofits' ethical behavior. Usually, ethics is viewed as related to the responsibility of making decisions according to a moral code. In nonprofit organizations, accountability implies not only a set of ethical standards, but also many other criteria that exceed these purely ethical standards.

Currently, ethical codes have become fashionable. They are necessary and significant, but they are hardly any more than a statement of good intentions that organizations adhere to. In other words, without strict compliance, they are worth as much as the paper they are written on. Accountability attempts to close the gap between good intentions and organizational facts. Therefore, ethics and accountability necessarily go hand in hand.

In short, as Kearns (1996: 40) states, accountability "means preserving the public's trust and, at the same time, keeping the promises made by organizations to their supporters, without departing from their mission and from adequate management practices."

Why Is It So Important for Nonprofits to be Transparent?

Thus, nonprofit organizations should try to escape from the natural inclination to report only financial matters and forget all other operational aspects. On the basis of Kearns' definition and what we have discussed so far, it is important to insist, yet again, on the fact that nonprofits' need to be transparent is not only associated with their efforts to raise funds from private donors, foundations, business companies and/or public administrations. On this regard, we should determine why transparency is so crucial for nonprofits. Five reasons surface as relevant (Figure 5.1):

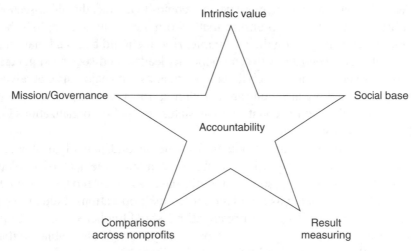

Figure 5.1   Reasons for accountability

Because It Is An Intrinsic Value for Operations

Transparent reporting to all internal and external stakeholders on organizational operations should become a dictum of all nonprofits. If volunteer organizations and foundations demand transparency and honesty from business companies and public administrations, they should be the ones to set the example. In short, integrity must become a core value.

The World Resource Institute

The World Resource Institute (WRI) is an organization devoted to environmental issues and is based in Washington, D.C. It recognizes integrity as one of its foundational values, along with innovation, promptness, independence and respect. For the WRI, values are not just rules, but a set of shared ideals that provide cohesion for the people working and collaborating with the organization. Together with the WRI mission, these values build the organization's identity and beliefs, shape its objectives, guide its actions and help explain its aspirations to others.

As regards integrity, the WRI states, "Our work must be candid and led by honesty, in order to guarantee our credibility and to earn the public trust." Within integrity, WRI people include the following operations:

1. "We invite our stakeholders to examine our methods, analyses and conclusions.
2. We share information and ideas with our colleagues and associates.
3. We acknowledge the contributions from those who offer their assistance." (http://www.wri.org/)

We tend to have a short memory when it comes to the fact that third-sector's capability to operate and to ensure that its organizations accomplish their mission depends largely on their own integrity. It should be noted that there is a sort of *social contract* between nonprofits leaders and society in general. By virtue of such "contract", civil society organizations enjoy special advantages other private organizations are not eligible for. However, these benefits are granted to them on account of their status as "public organizations" or "public service organizations".

As we explained in our introduction to the second part of the book, a distinctive feature in nonprofit organizations' management consists of its underlying values. Possibly, some nonprofits have not given enough thought to the core values that serve as foundation to all their operations. Indeed, some of the values that civil society organizations should adhere to at all times should include integrity, openness, accountability, service and public welfare (Jeavons, 2001). Accountability must be an intrinsic sector value, and, as such, nonprofits should incorporate it to their working habits.

Because It Allows Nonprofits to Acquire a Broad and Committed Social Base

A top priority for all nonprofit organizations should be to acquire a broad and committed social base – a large group of "activist" people who understand and unconditionally support their work. This goal may be attained only by thoroughly exposing organizations' workings and methods. Committed supporters need clear, concise and ongoing information. People who are averse to providing ongoing information on their organizations' achievements could argue that disclosure is costly, that it distracts money from the pursuit of their organizational missions. However, the reply to this argument is quite simple: all nonprofits missions also include the consolidation of a committed social base.

Because It Forces Nonprofits to Measure Their Results

Obviously, to report and explain results, it is necessary to measure them first. Whenever we refer to result measuring, two phrases come in handy: "Measure everything done" and "Accounting counts". Jim Rough (1998), member of one of the world's largest development NGOs, the American CARE, pointed out how difficult it was to measure results in many projects. He illustrated his point with an example of a development project:

A *food-for-work* project employs one thousand people to install a water distribution network. Workers share the food with their families, estimated at five individuals each. When the water system is up and running, it will benefit ten thousand local residents. How many direct beneficiaries should be calculated for this program? One thousand, six thousand, ten thousand, or sixteen thousand?

Surely, there is no single answer to this puzzling question, but civil society organizations should agree on a way to measure results in projects such as this – and many others, as well – in order to provide consistent replies and to compare the results of their various operations, analyzing the actual impact of each one of them.

The Charities Aid Foundation

The Charities Aid Foundation (CAF) is a non-governmental organization based in the United Kingdom that offers specialized financial services to other nonprofit organizations and their partners and associates. With over seventy-five years of experience and a global network that expands across five continents, the CAF primarily intends to increase the resources available for third-sector organizations, helping individuals and companies to enhance their "generosity's" value added. Periodically, the CAF compares several domestic organizations using various ratios – one of the most common ones being "fund-raising and administrative costs to overall expenses", in which a ratio over 20% is deemed unacceptable (CAF, 1998). (http://www.cafonline.org/)

Because It Helps Leaders to Monitor Compliance with Organizational Mission

Most nonprofits are managed on the basis of their projects and programs. These projects and programs shape future operations. Thus, the sector is rendered dysfunctional, since people manage organizations and foundations according to their own actions and not according to their results and missions. If an organization clearly exposes its results, it will check whether – or not – it is actually pursuing – and fulfilling – its mission.

A significant task for nonprofits' strategic leaders, as we will discuss in our next chapter, devoted to civil society organizations' governance, involves guiding the people who work in their organizations to measure their results and, essentially, the overall organizational impact on society.

Accountable on What and To Whom?

Accountability takes many forms. It may, for example, be *formal* – evaluating specific program results to determine whether preset objectives have been accomplished through program activities – or *informal* – based on regular feedback from other organizations and supporting institutions. Accountability may also involve a *functional approach* – to explain how organizations have used their resources and to review their action's direct impact – or a *strategic approach* – to measure operating results as related to organizational missions and society's current conditions. Finally, accountability may involve *upward reporting* – to donors, board members, public administrations and so on – or *downward reporting* – to beneficiaries, collaborators, users, personnel and so on.

The idea is that organizational accountability options are many and vary according to topics, addressees and formats. Clearly, the larger the nonprofit, the more explaining it will have to do, and the more organizations grow, the more transparent they need to be.

Accountability Areas for Nonprofits

This chapter does not intend to explore in detail the aspects of nonprofits' operations that should be accounted for. Each nonprofit organization constitutes a world of its own, and its leaders should exercise their own discretion to determine the topics the organization should report on to society.

In general terms, we could outline five large areas nonprofits should report on:

1. *Fiscal/financial area.* Nonprofits should be held accountable for their use of received contributions and their mechanisms to fulfill their legal obligations.
2. *Management area.* In this regard, nonprofit organizations should prove their use of adequate managerial procedures and personnel according to effectiveness and efficiency criteria.
3. *Operating area.* Volunteer organizations should explain how they carry out their operations and projects to prove their efforts to assure top quality and maximum results for users/beneficiaries.
4. *Top management area.* Nonprofits should also report on the composition of their governance bodies, informing who their leaders and workers are.

5. *Strategic area*. Finally, third-sector organizations should prove they focus their operations on the most relevant aspects of their missions, trying to contribute the most to society in their fields.

To Whom?

To whom should nonprofits report to? The answer to this question is not an easy one. Figure 5.2 (Vernis, 1999a) tries to outline some of the groups and people to whom nonprofit organizations should account to for their operations. In its inner section, we find organizations' internal stakeholders, as well as their immediate collaborators. This section involves the closest form of accountability. The outer section includes a series of organizations and foundations that should also be considered as relevant information recipients.

As we will explain in further detail in the next chapter, accountability is a responsibility of organizations' board of directors or trustees, who should report to society at large. Nonprofits' governance bodies are in charge of reporting organizational accomplishments. However, since daily activities in nonprofits are run by retained and volunteer staff, these individuals must

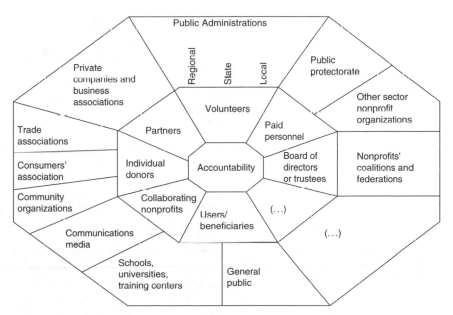

Figure 5.2   Inside and outside stakeholders for organizational accountability

report to boards – as established by most civil society organizations by-laws – and to users/beneficiaries. If these two groups are not fully aware of nonprofits' operations, then nonprofits will hardly be able to report to other internal and external stakeholders.

Let us establish, then, that each organization's accountability map is unique and complex, since each group of stakeholders requires a specific set of information. Nonprofits must explain their operations to their ongoing supporters, partners or members, as well as to their one-time donors. In addition, organizations should not forget the other organizations that collaborate with them in specific programs or projects. And, if organizations receive funding from public administrations, they should account for their operations, since those funds actually come from the entire population. In Figure 5.3, we have tried to map organizations' primary accountabilities. It would be interesting for organizations to map, using this example as a model, their own accountabilities.

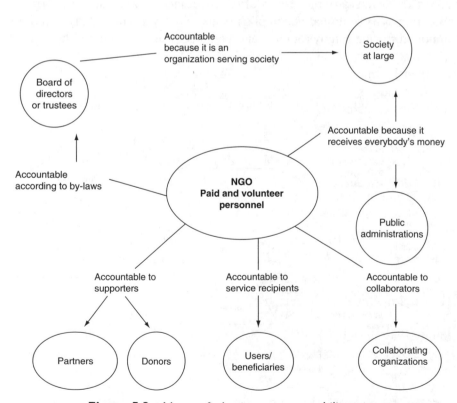

Figure 5.3   Nonprofits' primary accountability map

Accountability Mechanisms

Clear, systematic and attractive reporting on nonprofit operations is not an inexpensive endeavor. For younger and smaller organizations, which have limited resources and lack a sizable budget for communications or an expert to handle these matters, accountability costs may bear a significant impact. The funds and time allocated by each organization to the elaboration and publication of annual reports, newsletters, websites and mailings to partners and collaborators could be otherwise invested in the development of new projects addressing the needs of primary beneficiaries. In fact, spending on accountability may even drive some donors to cease contributing to an organization they feel is spending too much on communications.

Our advice to nonprofits on this regard is to find a fair balance between society's demand for more transparent nonprofits and the economic costs incurred by these efforts. Yet, present information technologies provide high-potential, low-cost tools that warrant a great impact. It is also necessary to consider the means and frequency used to disseminate this information. Accountability reporting should be viewed as a service and should be provided regularly to organization supporters either through annual reports or through newsletters. Currently, nonprofits' websites offer another inexpensive means to inform stakeholders. Accountability reports should be clear and easy to read, avoiding the use of technical jargons. If possible, they should include comparative charts and tables to plot, for example, year-to-date data versus previous years or periods.

In short, all nonprofits should regularly account for their operations. First, they should report their results to their own workers and direct collaborators. This procedure not only enhances motivation, but also provides an opportunity for associates to suggest possible improvements. Secondly, nonprofits should report to all external stakeholders, offering clear and transparent information, to ensure their continued support in the future.

Measuring Results: A Must for Accountability

Surely, we all agree that, in order to report activities initiated and their results over a specific period of time to collaborators and society in general, it is necessary to have a result measurement system in place. At the beginning of the chapter, we stated how hard it is to measure nonprofits' results, as compared to companies' and public administrations' results.

For several years, the nonprofit sector equaled result measurements to financial transparency, listing undertaken projects, a few quality standards and offering some information to beneficiaries. Then, in the 1990s, it became apparent that these management controls measured only the efforts undertaken for a specific group of people but did not assess whether those efforts had indeed produced any changes for them.

In recent years, there has been significant progress in measuring nonprofits' results, especially in fields such as international cooperation, where tools such as management by objectives have become regular features either because the organizations have been willing or forced – by funding agencies – to adopt them. At the same time, *ex post* evaluations are increasingly common for civil society organizations programs. In fact, some nonprofit organizations are already moving in that direction. Figure 5.4 may be helpful to understand the various organizational aspects that can be measured.

First, nonprofit organizations should measure their revenues or resources – financial, as well as material and human. Measuring revenues is fairly easy: it involves, for example, counting the funds received, rigorously registering their origin – individual donors, partners, public donors, own revenues and so on – as well as the number of volunteer hours, volunteers, specific goods used in operations and so on. Secondly, nonprofits can easily measure their projects and actions. For each project, organizations should specify their actions as related to their predetermined objectives. Measuring undertakings (outputs) is also relatively easy – and very important. For example, a nonprofit may count the number of families served by the health-care center or school funded.

In any case, problems arise when organizations try to measure their results (outcomes). Thus, to continue with the health-care center example, perhaps this nonprofit can measure the center's consultation rate or the

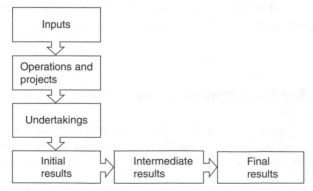

Figure 5.4 Nonprofits' value chain (*Source*: Elaborated by authors)

local community's disease reduction rate. However, this health-care center is, certainly, just one of the components of the nonprofit's long-term goals – probably summarized as "improving health conditions in a specific constituency" or "contributing to the development of a specific region". How should long-term results be measured? How can we evaluate organizational impact when it refers to better living standards? Again, not an easy question to answer.

Still, nonprofit organizations should try to measure their results. Maybe, a distinction between initial, intermediate and final results provides a suitable approach, as we show in Table 5.1.

Weighing organizations' actual results – their real impact – demands a sizable effort. That is why it is so important to clearly determine nonprofits' missions. Going back to the example of an organization working with the homeless, if its mission is defined as "offering a permanent home to the homeless", this nonprofit will have to measure its impact on very specific terms – for instance, based on "the number and share of beneficiaries who have regular living accommodations". Instead, if its mission is defined as "preventing the homeless from living in the streets", its impact will have to be measured in a completely different way – perhaps as related to the "number and share of beneficiaries who have spent 50 percent less nights on the street". These two different missions require two different ways to measure organizational impact.

Table 5.1	Example of result measurements for an organization working with the homeless
Inputs	Number of social workers
	Number of volunteers
	Number of one-time donors
Operations	Funded shelter overnight stays
	Funded meals at restaurants
Outputs	Number of people who go to the shelter out of the city's total homeless population
Initial outcomes	Number of people who go to the shelter on a regular basis
Intermediate outcomes	Number of people who embark on a specific program to recover habits
Final outcomes	Number of participants with regular accommodations

In a survey carried out in the United States (Hatry, van Houten, Plantz and Greenway, 1996), civil society organization officials who had successfully measured organizational results pointed out that a clear definition of results

- helps organizations to *focus their operations*;
- serves as an organizational *barometer*;
- offers valuable information to *improve programs* and to corroborate whether improvements actually yield expected results;
- turns into a highly useful *motivational tool* for organizations' employees and volunteers, and
- outlines organizations' *positioning* in their communities.

Summing up, the message we are trying to convey here is that, to fulfill their missions, nonprofit organizations should be able to measure, somehow, the impact of their operations on their constituencies. Only by candidly and honestly analyzing their results will they be able to determine whether they have been successful or not, what programs should be furthered in the future, which ones should be forgone and what new projects should be promoted.

Nonprofits' Benchmarking and Accountability

When we talk about transparency, one of the salient concerns for nonprofit leaders revolves around the reaction of supporters when they become aware of organizations' administrative expenses. The expenses that are not directly associated with program or project benefits are usually viewed as "superfluous" or, even, "unnecessary". Accordingly, nonprofits should explain to society at large that their administrative expenses are necessary to secure their objectives.

A more proactive attitude from civil society organizations in this regard should not be endorsed by a single organization. As has been the case in other countries, a coordinated, sector-wide effort is called for to educate donors on the need for administrative costs to ensure nonprofits' livelihood. Nonprofit benchmarking may be very helpful to remedy this situation. Indeed, it is the fourth element in our discussion on accountability.

We believe it is interesting to briefly dwell on the effort undertaken by the Charities Aid Foundation (CAF) in its *Benchmarking Charity Costs* study (Sargeant and Kaehler, 1998), which compares the administrative costs of five hundred UK nonprofits. Sargeant and Kaehler (1998: 7) use two specific indicators – "fund-raising costs" and "administrative costs" – as the basis of their study. Fund-raising and communications costs are "expenses incurred to drive others to make voluntary contributions to the organization". These costs may include advertising and direct marketing expenses, as well as payments made to people who act as fund-raisers for the organization. Administrative costs "include expenses associated with organizational management and operations", such as administrative, accounting and financial expenses, as well as the staff assigned to organizational management – and not to a specific program or project – and the expenses relating to legal and by-law requirements – board meetings, assemblies, audits and so on.

Based on both definitions, the CAF survey uses three benchmarking ratios: "administrative and fund-raising costs" (AFRC) to overall expenses ratio, "fundraising costs" (FR) to overall expenses ratio, and "administrative costs" (AC) to overall expenses ratio. Table 5.2 shows the results of these three ratios in 410 nonprofits for the 1992–1996 period.

In an interesting contribution, this study provides the ratio mean for surveyed nonprofits over a four-year period (1992–1996). Administrative and fund-raising costs have gone from accounting for 19.51 percent of overall expenses in 1992 down to 17.75 percent in 1996. This seems to indicate that surveyed nonprofits are making a solid effort to reduce their administrative costs.

Naturally, these nonprofits differ greatly, and the study tries to determine the reasons for these discrepancies. First, reasonably enough, there are significant differences between large and small nonprofits. Economies of scale have a remarkable bearing on AFRC – as the report points out, "small is beautiful, but also expensive". Additionally, nonprofit sub-sectors also exhibit relevant differences: for example, the study reveals an 8.8 percent administrative ratio for development NGOs, a 9 percent administrative ratio for health-related nonprofits, while this ratio climbs to 12.1 percent and 12.2 percent for social and miscellaneous nonprofits, respectively.

Table 5.2   Administrative and fund-raising costs

AFRC, AC and FR ratio means, 1992–1996	%
Administrative and fundraising costs	18.2
Fundraising costs	7.8
Administrative costs	10.4

Source: CAF, 1998.

Significant conclusions may be drawn from this study undertaken by the CAF in the United Kingdom:

- First, despite the widespread initial reluctance caused by the process itself, nonprofits ultimately recognize the need to benchmark their expenses.
- Secondly, measuring results is indeed costly, both in time and money, but, in the long run, it is the only way to assess the true impact of organizations.
- Thirdly, since external benchmarking systems afford very limited value, they should emerge from a coalition of nonprofit organizations.

Let us consider another interesting example – that of the *Fundación Lealtad* in Spain. Its mission has been defined as "promoting individual and corporate trust in organizations and foundations devoted to social assistance, development cooperation and humanitarian relief". To this end, and in line with our discussion so far, this foundation emphasizes the amount and quality of information available to the general public. Its work, rather than involving organizational audits and listings, focuses on three premises:

1) creating and funding a global and independent communication tool (the transparency and best practices guide), updated and user-friendly for current and potential donors;
2) reporting to society on civil society organizations situation through publications and contacts with the media; and
3) working with civil society organizations to improve their management practices, especially zeroing in on transparency.

Over 100 organizations, which account for 30 percent of the overall budget for social aid and development cooperation in Spain, have willingly agreed to be subject to *Fundación Lealtad*'s scrutiny. A complete report on each of these nonprofits is readily available at the foundation's website.

Table 5.3 summarizes the four primary transparency and best practice principles used by *Fundación Lealtad* to assess nonprofit organizations.

Table 5.3   *Fundación Lealtad's* transparency and best practice principles
1. Governance body operation and regulation principle   A. Governance bodies will consist of at least five members. B. Governance bodies will meet at least twice a year. These meetings will be attended by the majority of governance body members. C. All governance body members will attend at least one meeting every year.

	D. Only a limited number of governance body members will receive any form of compensation – always in accordance to current laws and never in excess of 40 percent. E. Governance body members will be reelected on a regular and pre-established basis. F. Names and brief CVs of governance members will be made public. G. Governance bodies will prove the existence of selection criteria for projects, suppliers, personnel and partner organizations to prevent conflicts of interest and discrimination. Organizations will also have a specific policy for dealings with business companies. These criteria and policies will be made public.
2. Social purpose clarity and exposure principle	A. The social purpose of an organization will be its primary goal. It will reflect on its operations, which should pursue a social interest. B. The social purpose will be clearly defined, identifying the organization's field of operations and its intended constituency. C. It will be known to all organization members, including volunteers. D. It will also be readily available to the general public.
3. Operation planning and monitoring principle	A. Organizations will have a formal planning to suit their operations and measurable objectives. Objectives associated with the project area will be made public. B. All plans will have to be approved by governance bodies. C. Programs will follow a specific work plan over, at least, three years. D. Programs will feature formal control and objective evaluation systems, including specific beneficiary identification. E. Project evaluation reports will be readily available for the general public.
4. Information communication and faithful representation principle	A. Advertising, fund-raising and public information campaigns will faithfully represent the organization's objectives and situation and will not be misleading in any way. B. The organization will indicate a priori potential donors and collaborators, actions and the media it will use to report on its operations. C. At least once a year, the organization will inform donors and collaborators on its operations. D. Efficient communications demand electronic mail and a proprietary operational website, which will be updated at least once a year. E. Economic and operating annual reports will be readily available, including a detailed statement of funding origins and destinations.

See other principles at http://www.fundacionlealtad.org.

Final Considerations

Once we have reviewed these elements – essential, in our opinion, to accountability – we would like to make a few final considerations in order to highlight some of the notions discussed and to introduce future reflection topics.

Accountability *is not a fad* currently sweeping the third sector on a global scale. Nonprofits' reporting is an intrinsic reflection of the sector's values and its "social contract" with society. *Nonprofits' future legitimacy will hinge on accountability.*

Nonprofit organizations should ponder on the significance of the various elements involved in accountability and their components. At the same time, we have to consider accountability as a flexible and dynamic exercise that enables younger organizations to focus only on responding to legal requirements, while more experienced organizations can work on several model factors, thus gradually improving their accountability skills. In short, there is no *single accountability recipe or format.*

Clear, accurate, continued and appealing nonprofit reporting is expensive. For smaller nonprofits, these costs bear a significant impact. Funds allocated to annual reports, newsletters, websites, e-mailing and bulletins are simply diverted from services to users/beneficiaries. *Nonprofit organizations should find an adequate balance between their desire to respond to society's demand for increased transparency and the economic costs entailed by these efforts.* Accountability is closely linked to fund-raising. It should be noted that *not* everything is fair in fund-raising. Nonprofits should adhere to ethical standards that encompass the various aspects of their fund-raising methodologies – namely, liaisons with companies, publicly portraying their program beneficiaries, marketing messaging and so on. *Transparency and ethics in fund-raising are also essential to preserve sector legitimacy.*

We should not forget nonprofit organizations are, for the most part, very young. They need time to improve their accountability skills – excessive criticism could actually "nip them in the bud". However, if accountability does not become a sector-wide practice, regularly and rigorously embraced, many organizations could end up being trapped in the past or failing to live up to their original missions. Thus, *a compromise should also be sought between accountability requirements and the average youth of sector organizations.*

An important part of noprofits' future accountability will also depend on an educated audience. Thus, *adequate media coverage for third-sector organizations will help them become more transparent.* As Morris (1998) appropriately states, civil society organizations and the media raise their independent voices to advocate public issues, and, as such, should be natural allies. Good media coverage would mean nonprofit sector existence beyond natural disasters and scandals, as an ongoing source of news.

The most complex accountability exercises are self-accountability. Indeed, there are two especially hard accountabilities in the third sector: Nonprofit executive directors' reporting to boards, and volunteers' reporting to paid employees. To avoid lengthy discussions, we have chosen to forgo their analysis in this chapter, but both deserve careful attention. Nonprofit governance has become a growing concern for the sector itself. How should retained officials be accountable to volunteer governance body members? At the same time, nonprofits recruiting large numbers of volunteers also require an additional kind of accountability: How should volunteers account for their specific actions to organization employees?

At a time when greater collaboration among nonprofits as well as real cross-sector partnerships with public administrations and businesses strongly emerge as urgent needs, accountability gathers increasing significance. As we claimed in the first section of this book, *collaborations among public, private, for-profit and nonprofit organizations demand further transparency from all players.*

Certainly, a way to improve nonprofit accountability would involve engaging the academic world, research foundations and other constituencies to *carefully analyze the third-sector situation.* Detailed studies focusing on this sector and its organizations will surely lead to its candid disclosure, so that it may be concluded that organizations withholding information indeed have something to hide. Benchmarking nonprofits in each sub-sector will also provide some interesting insights.

There is a clear danger that, if misconduct scandals break out in the nonprofit sector, public administrations will step in, firmly regulating the sector to prevent further abuse. Hence, it is very important for the third sector itself to anticipate any such situation by improving its accountability performance. Outside support to initiatives of this kind from foundations and/or public administrations may turn out to be instrumental. *Accountability efforts had better stem from a self-regulating drive from the sector itself and/or from collaborations with other organizations.*

Coupled with accountability, result measurements could help nonprofit organization leaders to come across very useful information on their operations. Thus, nonprofits should build adequate information systems and, subsequently, sort collected data in such a way as to prompt their leaders to embark on new strategic challenges. *Information is instrumental for nonprofit – or any other kind – organizations to continue innovating* (Drucker, 1999).

To conclude, nonprofits still have a long way to go in areas such as accountability, and they need time to improve their skills in this regard. The accountability challenge is fairly new to nonprofits around the world. Not so long ago, in the United Kingdom, Diana Leat (1996) provocatively wondered whether nonpofits should be held accountable. Several years later, this matter has become a core issue in debates on third-sector future. At a gathering of the world's ten largest development NGOs (Bellagio, 1999) that focused on their challenges resulting from globalization, one of the most outstanding internal challenges was defined as "the increasing demand for accountability, transparency and efficiency" (Lindenberg and Dobel, 1999). It should be noted, though, that, over the past few years, significant progress has been made in several nonprofits: they have started to report clearly and regularly to their collaborators and society on what they do, why and how they do it.

In any case, as we pointed out in our introduction, we should hold on to the notion that if we fail to turn accountability into a widespread practice in the third sector, many organizations will be stuck in the past or fail to fulfill their original missions. To rephrase one of our introductory statements, unless nonprofits provide society with truthful and candid information on their operations, in a rigorous and regular fashion, the trust society continues to deposit in them risks gradual impairment.

CHAPTER 6

Nonprofits' Governance Bodies and Governability

Introduction

One of the specific elements in nonprofit organizations that differentiates them from other private, for-profit and public organizations is the presence of volunteers in their governance bodies. Nonprofit boards' governance bodies include volunteer individuals who devote a portion of their time to leading social organizations.

People who work in the third sector know that governance bodies are having problems and difficulties in adjusting to the new demands in the nonprofit environment and specific tasks – which are becoming increasingly complex.[1] Some of the external factors have already been discussed in previous chapters, such as the various needs and challenges stemming from different social constituencies and requiring new approaches and cross-sector collaboration; the hurdles found in fund-raising, added to the logical uprising of the transparency culture; a new legal framework that sets the sphere, boundaries and format of nonprofit operations; the increasing need to raise society's trust in nonprofits; the keen attention of the media to NGOs and, perhaps, to third-sector headline-making misconduct. These outside factors, among others, are rendering nonprofits' environment growingly complex and, certainly, are exerting a strong pressure on third-sector governance.

The internal factors that prove third-sector governance maladjustments to this new reality include, among others, board members' lack of renewal[2] and poor dedication to the more strategic aspects of organizational leadership. Nonprofit organizations are often ruled by boards consisting of willing individuals whose terms continue year after year, without a clear focus on results. Many people who devote their time to nonprofits are involved in several organizations – which curtails their dedication to each one and their knowledge of their specificities.[3] In addition, these individuals are more concerned about everyday activities, lacking a medium- and long-term strategic vision of their organization or the preparation required to understand organizational quandaries and to contribute sound proposals.

As a result, nonprofit organizations are often governed by "well-meaning" people, with reduced availability and scarce leadership and representativeness, who are ill-equipped to bring effectiveness to governance roles. Thus, in the end, it is the same people who manage and lead nonprofits – the team of retained professionals (Carver, 1997).

An Approach to Several Types of Governance Bodies

We have just mentioned two of the key criteria needed to analyze the role of nonprofit governance bodies: first, member commitment and, second, leadership and representativeness. When we talk about commitment, we refer to the actual involvement of board members in their organizations and management. When we talk about leadership and representativeness, we refer to the value members may contribute to organizational governance, as well as to their legitimacy as people who are able to set the strategic course for the management team to follow.

These two factors – commitment and leadership, on the one hand, and representativeness, on the other – may be plotted into a matrix (Figure 6.1). Although it oversimplifies the real composition of governance bodies, this model will be helpful in our discussion of nonprofit boards.

Between the extremes we have dubbed *decorative* and *star governance bodies*, there is a wide range of possibilities. We have highlighted two: the *capable but unmotivated governance bodies*, consisting of people who could contribute greatly to their organizations, in terms of leadership and strategic vision, but lack the encouragement and motivation to fully live up to their role, and the *well-meaning governance bodies* – far more common – that include highly committed and motivated people – sometimes, from the management team itself – who are severely impaired to understand current environments and nonprofits' managerial needs and to exercise adequate leadership and representativeness.

Our reasons are obvious: third-sector capacity building – the core purpose of this book – necessarily calls for an in-depth revision of the governance role. To that end, we need to carefully analyze the tasks to be performed by each governance body, the most qualified individuals to partake in it and the best

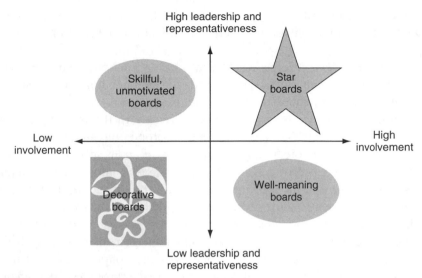

Figure 6.1 Analytical model of nonprofits' governance bodies. (*Source*: Elaborated by the authors)

way to renew them and to assess their work. Indeed, such are the objectives of this chapter.

Management and Governance

"There is a crucial difference between monitoring an organization's operations and actually undertaking them" (Mill, 1867: 100). "It is not fitting for the person who writes the laws to be the one to enforce them and for a group of people to shift the focus of their attention from general considerations to very specific terms" (Rousseau, 1762: 101).[4]

This double reference to the classics, Mill and Rousseau, should help us understand the difference between management and governance – two essentially different notions that are often confused not only in the field of nonprofits, but also in private and public organizations' management.

In a foundation or nonprofit organization, *governance* engulfs a series of notions or functions. In the first place, it encompasses tasks of a more strategic nature, such as mission definition, long-term planning, environmental demand interpretation and policy formulation. In the second place, it implies a set of functions associated with organizational resources, such as ensuring resource availability and financial sustainability, monitoring organizational performance and accounting for organizations' operations, as we discussed in the previous chapter. Finally, governance also involves leadership and a clear organizational vision (Bowen, 1994; Carver, 1997; Vernis *et al.*, 1998).

In turn, *management* refers to the decisions and actions associated with policy implementation, policy-based project organization, and resource coordination and utilization to attain preset objectives.

In short, governance – strategic level – relates to the primary options adopted by organizations to adjust to their environments. In other words, it refers, as we stated before, to the determination of and respect for organizations' primary, long-term goals and objectives, the adoption of suitable courses of action, and the medium- and long-term allocation of resources. Instead, management – at the operative level – refers to the execution of the guidelines set by the organization's governance heads. A common cause for the confusion between governance and management results from the inception and growth process undergone by many nonprofits. Oftentimes, the people who decide to create an organization are the same who determine its mission and objectives. Then, the same individuals also coordinate projects and activities, eventually assuming the whole responsibility for its daily operations. Thus, there is a functional overlapping of governance and management. Some management theoreticians specializing in organizational development stages, such as Greiner (1967), have referred to this phase as the inception or creation stage, characterized by the existence of a leader or group of leaders/founders who are in charge of everything, in an organization with minimal formal systems that reward innovation and relies directly on its creators or on their close oversight.

Light Bulbs and the Board

A while back, we were invited to join in the final moments of the monthly board meeting held at a nonprofit organization. We got there a little early, and the chairwoman asked us to listen in on the last part of the meeting, before our intended intervention. We were stunned to hear that the final item in the agenda was the substitution of energy-saving bulbs for the regular bulbs installed in the organization's premises. Six highly trained individuals – none of them a certified electrician – spent half an hour discussing whether the light bulbs should be changed or not!

However, a situation such as this should not repeat itself once the initial stage is over, when organizational survival is assured and it is possible to increase operations and to promote the people involved in them. Growth should bring more volunteers, who can take on some managerial tasks. In some cases, it may even afford organizations a chance to hire qualified personnel to support organizational management. In addition, this growth process could enable the initial group of volunteers to gradually focus exclusively in organizational governance.

Surely, those of us who devote our time to studying third-sector management have traditionally added to this confusion. We have written and taught on management issues, but we have failed to address nonprofit governance issues with sufficient depth and thoroughness.

We should understand how hard it is to distinguish between governance and management during organizations' early years, as well as for smaller organizations, which usually, as we have already pointed out, feature an overlapping of both functions. Also, we should recognize that it is very difficult to change the way in which people act. In other words, it is not easy for a board of directors or trustees that has historically managed an organization to stop doing that and focus primarily on organizational governance.

Although we are acutely aware of these hurdles, we believe the distinction between governance and management to be a mandatory requirement. If there is no governance and there is only management, foundations and nonprofits may end up focusing on survival and neglecting their missions. As we shall discuss momentarily, overseeing mission fulfillment is a key board task that pertains to governance and not to management.

Major Governance Body Responsibilities

Defining the exact role and tasks of nonprofit organizations' governance bodies is certainly no easy task.

In this section, we will try to deepen our understanding of governance body responsibilities to remedy the theoretical and analytical shortage we mentioned in our introduction to this chapter, where we referred to the rampant confusion between governance and management that plagues domestic nonprofits. To put it differently, we will explore the meaning of governance in nonprofit organizations.

Before we discuss the connotations of the word "governance" for nonprofit organizations, we should mention that Hodgkinson and Murray (1994) confirms three facts:

1. First, in nonprofits, governance bodies' responsibilities are *independent* from organizational features. In other words, governance bodies in nonprofits have *similar primary responsibilities* throughout the sector. In addition, these responsibilities are clearly set forth in organizations' by-laws.
2. Second, the way in which governance bodies fulfill these responsibilities *depends on several factors, such as organization type, size, background*

and/or evolution stage. For instance, governance responsibilities will be handled differently in a nonprofit start-up and in an organization with twenty-five years of experience.

3. Third, since organizations and their respective environments change over time, nonprofits are forced to *periodically review their governance structures.*

An additional factor must be added to the preceding three. As organizations develop and grow, their governance evolves, *shifting and fine-tuning governance body roles and responsibilities.* In other words, the chairman of a nonprofit start-up has different responsibilities and performs roles other than the chairman of a well-established organization.

After describing the factors molding governance body responsibilities, it is now possible to discuss what its primary responsibilities are.

Ensuring Mission Compliance and Organizational Value Preservation

Nonprofits' original missions and purposes may be modified only by governance bodies. It is a governance responsibility to ensure their pursuit. This self-evident statement is not really redundant, for an increasing number of nonprofit organizations do not seem to fully understand their purpose or simply stray from their initial missions.

We are not going to dwell, once again, on how important it is for nonprofits to have a clearly defined specific mission shared by all their internal and external stakeholders. Suffice it to say that this is the prerequisite for their missions to effectively guide all organizational operations.

Foundation to Assist the Homeless

The dilemma posed by "beds for mentally-ill patients" versus "beds for homeless patients": A foundation was about to build a small, thirty-bed shelter to assist the homeless. The shelter's primary objective was to provide accommodations for people in the streets who needed a place for long convalescences and would otherwise succumb to previous diseases. The board faced financial distress: the foundation had the building and the money to refurbish it, but it did not have the economic capacity to operate the shelter on a 24 hours, seven days a week schedule. The foundation's executive director presented the board with a solution through an agreement with the local public administration. The local government could fund fifteen beds, but they would have to be offered to mental patients. The director agreed to this condition, since many of the homeless people roaming the streets are, to begin with, mentally ill.

However, the board did not approve the director's proposal, arguing that the foundation's mission was to assist the homeless and the shelter was designed to provide a place for long convalescences. The foundation's mission was not to provide assistance to mental patients.

As the preceding example suggests, we should focus on the primary role of governance bodies to support and control mission compliance. Surely, in the case of the foundation that assisted the homeless, if the board had not carefully controlled mission relevance, in a few years, the foundation could have ended up deploying significant efforts and resources for activities that did not match its original purpose. Obviously, the organization's official was doing his job: as a retained employee, his foremost concern was to ensure the organization's long-term survival.

In short, as Berger and Poli (2000) accurately point out, a governance body "should periodically revise the organization's mission to ensure its relevance, adequacy, viability and feasibility and to make the necessary adjustments". Governance bodies must watch over their organizations' missions and underlying values. It is not an easy task, especially in increasingly complex environments, where fund-raising is also growingly difficult. The following document illustrates this point effectively.

A Free Video for a Foundation

A foundation's executive director received a video and a telephone call from a leading advertising agency. Unsolicited, the agency had produced an advertising video for the foundation and was now requesting its permission to broadcast it immediately on several movie theaters in the city. Taken a little aback by the agency's move, the foundation's head watched the video and, mildly satisfied with it, sent it to all board members for their approval. Unanimously, the board decided to reject the agency's proposal. The video did not portray the organization's values, depicting it as a group of professionals who cared about emergencies and "saving lives". Naturally, the footage was shocking, but it failed to convey any of the humane warmth, long-term dedication and volunteer work values the organization stood for.

If the board had reacted hastily, the video would have betrayed the organization's values. Instead of promoting the foundation, it would have upset the people who willingly supported the organization with their time or money – among other ill-effects.

Approving Organizations' Strategic or Action Plans

One of governance bodies' most significant contributions to assure nonprofits' sound operations involves devoting enough time to reflect on their organizations' future and the strategic options to be currently adopted in order to anticipate and influence environmental changes. This strategic planning process demands drawing away from organizations' everyday "business" to imagine the environment they will face in coming years. Usually, these reflections will be poured into a vision, a strategic plan for a number of years, and several action plans will derive from the latter.

Often, governance bodies have neither the time nor the capabilities required to formulate organizations' strategic plans. Still, they should not neglect their strategic thinking process, and they should ensure strategic plans are drawn, either by their organizations' management teams or with the support of an outside team retained to coordinate and facilitate the necessary analysis. Formulated plans should be submitted to governance bodies for their discussion and approval. Once plans have been adjusted and approved, they become a support tool for boards to perform their tasks, since they provide board members with a framework to guide organizational operations. Then, governance bodies need to focus on monitoring plan execution.

Strategic plans afford another advantage: they may be used to allocate organizations' scarce resources according to true priorities and organizational ideals. At the same time, strategic plans may help governance bodies to better understand organizational and environmental realities. Detailed analysis will drive organizations' key decision-makers to have enough quantitative and qualitative information, preventing the adoption of narrow-minded, partial, biased or excluding positions.

Finally, strategic plans also act as reinforcement mechanisms for governance bodies' institutional leadership. Indeed, during strategic plan elaboration processes, governance bodies will get to know better the internal and external stakeholders involved in their organizations' operations.

Ensuring Organizations' Economic Viability

Governance bodies should also try to have an active role in the formulation of their organizations' major financial strategies. Financial resources are usually very scarce and limited; thus, in order to broaden the scope of the operations involved in their processes and missions, organizations need to define specific funding strategies. Any demands to management teams for further actions and better results will always have to be supported by adequate financial resources.

A Reluctant Board

In the late 1990s, a domestic nonprofit organization devoted to promoting the American language and culture in Spain hired a new executive director from the United States. The newcomer, an entrepreneurial woman with vast knowledge on nonprofit operations, quickly realized that the organization was overseen by a board that would be of little help in raising the funds urgently needed to ensure its survival. The new director wanted to include officials from U.S. multinationals operating in Spain in the organization's board. However, she remained in office for less than a year: the members of the old board were very reluctant to leave their prestige-building positions.

It is true that many nonprofits have internal or external teams specializing in fund-raising activities. Usually, the larger the organization and its operations, the greater the efforts devoted to fund-raising, including specific teams and marketing departments. Even in these cases, governance bodies should also be actively involved in fund-raising. As Berger and Poli (2000) graphically put it, "give, get or get off". In other words, board members are expected to either make individual donations, obtain donations from other institutions and people through their networking efforts, or withdraw from organizational leadership.

Exercising Strategic Leadership to Build Trust

As we discussed in the previous chapter on accountability, third-sector growth cannot be sustained without building and keeping society's trust.

At the risk of repeating ourselves in our effort to convey a clear message to organizations, nonprofits must build trust. This means, first, ensuring all their actions match their organizational values and creating the necessary systems to guarantee their respect for these values. Second, building trust entails communicating their actions with rigor and transparency. These pursuits will not be possible without proper governance. In order for domestic nonprofits to be able to account for their actions candidly to society in the future, they need good governance and governability.

In any nonprofit organization, people usually determine the focus of their attention and energy. And, normally, these decisions are shaped by external pressures and the urgency of everyday operations. In this context, it is very hard to incorporate the notion of accountability in organizations' and foundations' workers because this issue is seldom urgent and there are always more pressing, immediate matters calling for their attention.

A primary and significant task for those in charge of strategic leadership in nonprofits involves helping organizations' employees understand that building trust is a priority for each and every one of their members or partners.

Another major task for governance body members in third-sector organizations hinges on acting as true organizational leaders. Performing this leadership role entails, among other things, the realization that the organization is *ultimately* under their control. In short, board members should perform the role of private business owners, which may not be delegated to manager or executive directors. We insist on the notion that governance body members are responsible for nonprofits before society.

A third task for nonprofits' governance bodies is associated with accountability and involves working to ensure their organizations measure the results of their operations, especially focusing on the assessment of their final impact on society. Governance bodies must monitor mission accomplishment and, to that end, they need to know the actual impact of their organizations and programs.

Recruiting Executive Directors

A crucial decision for the governance body of a fairly organized nonprofit involves the selection of the individual who will be responsible for the organization's executive management – the executive director, chief executive or general manager. It is not an easy decision, and part of its success depends on an accurate profiling of the position in terms of both its responsibilities and the key qualities and competencies required to manage the organization. Another paramount success factor in recruiting nonprofits' chief executives rides on the assessment of candidates' sensitivity for and synchronicity with each organization's values, mission and vision. Indeed, executive directors largely become the keepers of organizational cultures.

Governance bodies, especially in fairly established and resourceful organizations, may retain an outside recruiter for the initial candidate selection process or entrust the internal team with it. However, it is essential for the board to make the final call on any one candidate to manage the organization. The chief executive chosen will – along with the management team, if such were the case – be in charge of reporting on organizational operations to the board of directors or trustees. Thus, he or she should be fully trusted by the governance body.

As we shall discuss later, the relationship between the board and the person who runs the nonprofit is instrumental for organizational success. Not only should their respective duties be clearly defined and delimited, but there should also be an explicit system in place to evaluate the performance of both executive directors and paid management teams.

Assessing Their Own Performance

Last but not least important, nonprofits' governance bodies should be able to evaluate their own performance in order to establish, at all times, whether and how they are effectively living up to their responsibilities – which we have listed in this section. In other words, boards need a set of guidelines to determine whether the roles assumed by their members are duly performed.

Next, we suggest a number of basic questions for governance body members to answer once a year in order to assess their performance as effective nonprofits' boards.

- Does each and every one of the governance body members receive enough information on the organization's operations?
- At board meetings, are decisions made on specific issues associated with organizational governance or do members just receive information?
- At board meetings, do members regularly review the organization's operations?
- Does each governance body member have a specific task related to the organization's operations?
- Does the board periodically review some result measurements to assess the organization's actual impact?
- Does the board compare the organization's working methods, expense ratios and overall results to those of similar nonprofits?
- Does the board actively remind all members of organizational values, effectively watching over their preservation?
- Does the board periodically control the fulfillment of the organization's mission?

Governance Body Composition, Training and Renewal

Certainly, a crucial issue in the discussion of nonprofit sector governance bodies involves their composition. How should board members be recruited? Volunteer dedication to the board of directors of a nonprofit organization or the board of trustees of a foundation implies a significant time investment. Finding the people who are willing to devote their time to a nonprofit is not an easy job.

Traditionally, in the nonprofit world, the individuals who have participated in boards are the same who have been directly involved in the lives of their organizations. These people know their organizations' daily operations very well because they have been there. Thus, it is very common for restless youngsters to join the boards of their youth associations in their desire to do more than volunteer work over the weekend. Or, in environmental organizations, biologists and veterinarians often join the boards to embrace their love for nature also during their leisure time. However, the problem is that the competencies or type of dedication required to teach children on weekends are not the same as those demanded to govern a youth organization. Naturally, the same goes for environmental organizations and their volunteers.

The process to build an organization's board should start with a revision of its current and future needs. Yet, oftentimes, the process is reversed: a group of people are willing to take on organizational responsibilities, and, then, through inner power balances, the board of directors or trustees comes together. This method reveals a significant lack of strategic vision.

As the recruiting process for a company's management team is increasingly becoming a carefully planned task that involves retaining external consultants, nonprofit organizations' board composition should also be carefully planned with utmost professionalism and strategic vision. Solid planning before recruiting governance body members will prevent future organizational problems. Berger and Poli (2000) recommend a five-step procedure to build a board for a nonprofit organization:

1. Setting the selection criteria for new members and clearly defining adequate profiles.
2. Identifying candidates with suitable conditions.
3. Raising – and nourishing – the interest of potential candidates.
4. Recommending selected candidates to whom it may concern – assembly or board – according to the provisions of organizational by-laws.
5. Introducing and orienting new members on their responsibilities as governance body participants.

A basic notion derived from these steps indicates that it is increasingly necessary to seek potential candidates for governance bodies in circles outside the groups closely related to the organization. Organizations need "fresh blood": new ideas, outlooks and approaches, different ways to view the organization and its relationship with its environment and so on. If we restrain ourselves to seeking people already attached to the organization, we will be likely to find candidates who will make very few new contributions to our operations. Such is the case of organizations that may be categorized as endogamous or wrapped-up in themselves; these organizations risk stagnation and the rejection of any ideas or proposals coming from the outside.

Naturally, this proactive search outside the traditional organizational boundaries renders the boards' composition and renewal processes more complex and resource-intensive – especially time-wise. Hence, it is important to "cultivate" potential candidates. Their interest in our organization will not be sparked by a mere telephone call. Indeed, it will take time to build the mutual trust required – for the organization to trust the candidate and vice versa. Thus, governance body changes take time, especially to wait for the right candidates "to surface".

So, what kind of candidates are we looking for? It is important for nonprofit organizations to seek people with different profiles and backgrounds, whose diverse knowledge will enrich the organization's vision. Governance body diversity molds not only its internal dynamics but that of the entire organization, profiting from the various viewpoints of people from different backgrounds. Of course, it is difficult for someone from the nonprofit sphere and someone from the business sector to "speak the same language", but, if they manage to "speak the language of the organization", then they will be able to jointly embark on new paths to improvements. In addition, cross-generation relations and cross-cultural work will be hard to navigate; still, as we have said before, we believe the nonprofit world needs to open up its boards to "fresh blood".

One of the steps recommended by Berger and Poli (2000) for governance composition and often neglected is the orientation new board members should receive. It should be noted that, once an individual has joined a governance body, he/she will need some training or updating on several essential issues to fully perform the role he/she has assumed. We refer to issues such as the organization's background, its specific challenges or difficulties, especially when new members come from the outside. They should familiarize themselves with the organization's strategic plan and foremost action plans; they should meet several organization members, including employees, volunteers and stakeholders – donors and so on. This process will demand additional time and dedication at first.

Finally, we should also bear in mind that nonprofits undergo a particularly critical phase when they face governance body renewal – that is, when a governance team concludes its term and it is time for a new team to step in. This transition should be anticipated and planned for. Former board members are key players, whose historical and institutional memory deserves preservation. Their experiences may come in handy for newcomers, who will thus avoid repeating mistakes, understand past processes and ensure continuity. Organizations must try to keep these individuals close to their operations. In other words, organizations and their leaders have a twofold responsibility in governance:

1. On the one hand, they need to ensure that the knowledge accumulated by former board members is effectively transferred to the organization in order to prevent experience losses.
2. On the other hand, they should keep in touch with former board collaborators – for instance, through providing regular information on a quarterly or annual basis – because the organization is likely to need their help once again in the future.

Some organizations prefer partial governance body renewals to ensure the ongoing presence of incumbents with several years of experience, in combination with the arrival of new members. For example, boards may be renewed by halves or thirds in order to assure governance continuity. In fact, some organizations resort to assigning "mentors" to newcomers (Carver, 2001).

Another way to assure the presence of knowledgeable governance body members is to establish short terms, although board assignments should be long enough to allow members to acquire an in-depth knowledge of organizational operations, and yearly renewal. Also, nonprofits' chairmen may send letters to board members to remind them of their responsibilities and commitments.

Finally, we feel it is important to reinforce the notion that being part of a governance body implies a commitment to the organization that should be honored. This is a twofold commitment that requires taking the following aspects into account:

- Clearly detailing the dedication expected from board members.
- Setting specific objectives for each board member (specific dedication and responsibilities) and periodically assessing performance.
- Finding ways to optimize the use of governance members' time and knowledge, avoiding any form of abuse and sticking to their original assignment.
- Creating a working dynamics between the management team and the board – for instance, through the appointment of ad hoc committees for specific, urgent issues (change management, fund-raising, organizational positioning and image, etc.).
- Building support teams for the governance body – for example, task forces, advisory committees and so on.
- Installing the necessary systems to ensure ongoing communications that flow both ways and the unfaltering respect for transparency and accountability standards.

Table 6.1 Sample test on governance body performance	
Test on governance body performance to be answered individually by board members	
Rate the following statements on a 1–5 scale, where 5 means you strongly agree with the statement, 4 means you agree with the statement, 3 means you partially agree with the statement, 2 means you disagree with the statement, and 1 means you strongly disagree with the statement.	Score number (5, 4, 3, 2 or 1)
Statements on board meetings:	
I believe annual meetings allow for an adequate monitoring of the organization's operations.	
I prepare in advance for board meetings, thus improving their development.	
Board meetings are dynamic and interactive; the agenda is discussed freely, and decisions are made by consensus.	
In general, board meetings are highly productive.	
Statements on the information received by board members:	
…	
Statements on board duties:	
…	
Statements on board composition:	
…	
Statements on board renewal:	
…	
Statements on the relationship of the board with the organization's executive director:	
…	
Statements on organizational mission accomplishment:	
…	
Statements on the respect for organizational and sector values:	
…	
Statements on your role as board member:	
…	
Statements on the course of organization's operations	
…	

Source: Elaborated by the authors.

Conclusions

Throughout this chapter, we have insisted on the relevance of governance bodies for nonprofits' capacity building. If we want the third sector to move forward at the speed required by relational society, it should be led by people who are fully aware of the crucial significance of their role.

To put it differently, the third sector needs less *decorative* and *well-meaning boards*, as we anticipated in our introduction to this chapter, and more *star boards*, whose members are fully involved in the definition of their organizations' strategic course, with large doses of leadership and representativeness.

As an epilogue to this chapter, we believe there are several basic questions boards should ask themselves to assess whether they are performing adequately. Mostly, these questions will lead governance body members to explore new ways to enhance their involvement. This is just an outline, since each organization should draft its own list of questions. We have designed this questionnaire as a quiz to "test" boards (Table 6.1).

CHAPTER 7

The Human Team

Introduction

The greatest asset of nonprofit organizations lies in their people. It is safe to say that, regardless of their access to economic resources, they find their key to success in a prepared and committed human team.

However, despite its critical nature, many organizations today do not have explicit policies to manage their people. This accounts for a major concern in a sector in which both volunteer and full-time workers' skills and commitment is instrumental. Although, of course, there are other relevant components, service value directly depends on the training and motivation of the people delivering it. Thus, nonprofit organizations owe it to their users and to society at large – for supporting and trusting them – to develop and strengthen their human teams.

In this task, as we shall discuss later, each organization plays a leading role, but the entire sector, public administrations and private companies also have a helpful and highly relevant function. We should not forget that, although skillful and committed human teams are a prerequisite for influential organizations – a key factor to consolidate the nonprofit sector's place in society – sector consolidation and the existence of well-structured and effective organizations, in turn, largely determine social and volunteer workers' training and commitment. Hence, in this issue, we find a sort of mutual feedback among its elements, in which the involvement of outside agents may also be significant (Figure 7.1).

Skillful human teams, efficient organizations and a high-impact sector become, then, even more relevant to the setting we have outlined. The increasing number of services outsourced by public administrations, as we viewed in Chapter 3, and the growing competition with private companies in these areas challenge nonprofits to prove their effectiveness and

Figure 7.1   Relations among these three levels

distinctive value. In this new scenario, personnel competency and commit-ment turn crucial. On the one hand, the emergence of new social demands and the need for sector organizations to perform a clearly defined role as public awareness and social outcry drivers enhance the promotion of new competencies, stressing the requirement for nonprofits' personnel to develop sector-specific abilities.

We are referring to all levels of nonprofits' personnel structures: boards (see Chapter 6), management teams, administrative positions, technicians and frontliners – in direct contact with users. Despite the diverse nature and responsibilities of these jobs, we believe organizational long-term success hinges on adequate training and commitment at all levels.

What Does It Mean to Have a Skillful Team?

It seems obvious, then, that skillful and committed human teams amount to a key requirement to understand the role and impact of nonprofits organizations in society. Still, what does it take to have a skillful team? How can an organization tell if its human team is adequate?

A primary sign that indicates how skilled and committed volunteer or full-time workers are lies in their efficiency to perform their respective tasks. When we talk about efficiency or effectiveness, we refer to the ability to achieve preset objectives by using adequate procedures and proc-esses. Thus, in order to evaluate workers' effectiveness and to collect information on their skills, nonprofit organizations should work with clearly defined jobs, responsibility assignments, preset objectives and action-guiding criteria – all these requirements are currently neglected by many organizations.

Fund-raisers must be clear on whether volunteer team maintenance and enhancement are part of their job objectives. If they are not provided with this basic information, they may deploy the wrong competencies. Thus, communications become a key factor.

Adjusting Objectives

Objectives and procedures should be carefully set and fine-tuned to prevent the risk of evaluating efficiency according to inadequate criteria. Is it efficient for an organization to have a fund-raiser who manages to increase private funding 2% above forecast, but forces the desertion of all fund-raising team volunteers? Does this individual hold all the competencies required to efficiently perform his/her job? The answer to this question depends on the significance of this team of volunteers and its potential value for each organization.

Hence, efficient performance would indicate that an organization's personnel are suitably prepared to undertake their tasks. However, the opposite is not necessarily true, for efficient job performance rides not only on the skills of individual workers, but also on the job's design and specific features, as well as on the organizational environment where it is performed (Figure 7.2).

From this viewpoint, as pointed out by Boyatzis (1982), competencies are necessary but not sufficient for organizations to secure workers' desirable performance. Also required are adequate organizational structures; good working conditions, ensured by suitable promotion, training, hiring and compensation policies; coherent job descriptions, grouping tasks in a rational fashion on the basis of specific organizational structures that suit environmental conditions as well as workers' type (volunteer and full-time),

Figure 7.2   Efficiency model. (*Source*: Boyatzis, 1982)

availability and commitment; and clearly defined responsibilities and objectives. Again, the close relationship between organizations and people comes forth strongly: skillful people not only manage effective organizations but also require organizations that fill that bill as well.

This issue involves one of the foremost challenges nonprofits must face if they pursue long-term consolidated impact: carefully reviewing their organizational structures and the roles played by their stakeholders. This review should incorporate the design of training, recruiting, job description, promotion, development, involvement and communications policies that match organizational objectives.

A Social Organizational Hires a New Executive

The new recruit seems to have all the competencies required for the job. She knows the sector and is renowned in it as well, since she has worked as managing director of a very similar organization. She has managerial experience and knowledge, has shown great initiative and driven the organization she used to run to grow significantly, undertaking innovative projects. She interacts well with people, and the teams she has overseen appreciate her as a good leader.

The newcomer enthusiastically joins the organization. There is a lot to be done in this organization. She is very committed at first, but she finds a complex organization, with aged personnel and a highly conservative culture. Changes are very hard to introduce. Any minor improvement takes such a toll that, by the end of the first six months, the executive has already compromised half of her change expectations. By the end of her first year in the new organization, she decides the situation is hopeless and starts looking for a new job.

What happened? Did the new hire have the competencies required? Where did she go wrong? Would another person have managed to make the necessary changes? Organizational maturity and features mold the impact of certain competencies. In this case, the organization was not ready to be managed by an executive with this profile. Despite her qualifications, her competencies were useless in this organization.

This reflection should also enable organizations to define the type of personnel they require and to determine the specific competencies their workers should possess in order to perform efficiently.

Human teams' required skills and commitment – necessary competencies – in nonprofits and foundations will vary across organizations. In addition, as we have already pointed out, team efficiency will not only depend on these two elements – though they are certainly indispensable. Along these lines, and far from neglecting the significance and the connection of the above-mentioned elements, we would like to further explore the topic of competencies. Thus, we will try to explain what competencies mean, listing some generic competencies that pertain to most nonprofits' staffs, as well as introducing some of the mechanisms used by organizations to drive skill acquisition.

What Do We Mean When We Refer to Competencies?

"Competencies" are characteristics that result from efficient or outstanding performance by a human being in his/her job (Klemp, 1980). Thus, competencies relate to the individual or collective ability to perform a specific task.

Competencies stem from the interaction between individuals' own features – personality traits and specialized expertise – and their motivations, images and social networks. Indeed, competencies result from joining two dimensions: an objective dimension, associated with individual characteristics, and a subjective dimension, related to the value assigned by individuals to specific aspects, as well as their own and others' perception of their personality and behavior. The latter dimension – scantily disseminated as yet – provides a key to determine the impact of individuals' characteristics on their behavior. Indeed, it is just as important, for example, for nonprofits' executives to be qualified for making decisions and meeting challenges – their own trait – as for their employees to believe they can do it – social role. This is a key feature in competency design and a typical source of misuse. The enumeration of required abilities for effective job performance should include not only their innate or acquired features – personality traits and knowledge – but also their subjective value. When we consider a specific competency, both objective and subjective elements required by that competency should be taken into account. Thus, it is possible to map the necessary characteristics for each job. Clearly, these features will have to be prioritized and will serve as standards to recruit and select candidates, and also – and foremost – to train the people who make up organizations' human teams.

A competency is a personal characteristic that results from a combination of some of the following elements: personality traits, specialized knowledge, motivation, self-image and social role.

- Personality traits: general response to events.
- Specialized knowledge: acquired through prior training or working experiences.

- Motivation: concern for a specific issue or goal, something moving individuals.
- Self-image: individuals' assessments about themselves.
- Social role: how others perceive an individual's behavior and his/her place in society.

Next, we present an example for a fund-raiser in Table 7.1:

Transformations in Competency Type and Level Required

As we have stated, each nonprofit requires specific competencies. However, considering recent environmental changes and the new challenges they will bring about, we provide a list of some of the major transformations that will reshape the type and level of competencies required by these organizations.

Increased strategic competencies and resourcefulness for almost all organizational levels

In an increasingly competitive environment, where needs change rapidly, organizational survival will no longer hinge on knowing how to do well what we usually do, but on knowing how to expand, adjust and innovate those operations. At all organizational levels, this innovation will demand a greater environmental analysis capability, thorough knowledge of organizations' conditions – full awareness of their potential and limitations – as well as the ability to design suitable action strategies. Initiative, innovativeness, the ability to take on further responsibilities and to embrace a deeper commitment to organizational causes and projects – beyond the specific call of duty – will also become crucial.

Being in charge of setting the strategic course of organizations, trustees and board members, as we said in the previous chapter, will need, more than ever before, a great ability to anticipate the future, to spot opportunities and to promote organizations' desired positioning. In turn, this positioning will demand further involvement from organizational members. Thus, their social role will be instrumental inside the organization, as well as their ability not only to formulate projects but also to communicate them. Similarly, organizations' management teams, being the major source of information for governance bodies, will be forced to strengthen their analysis capability and their ability to communicate with them.

Table 7.1 Fund-raisers' competency profile

Competency	Motivation: desires	Personality traits	Knowledge: know-how	Self-image	Social role
Ability to take on tough challenges (human)	Tough challenges	Ability to endure failure or hardship Optimism Initiative		High self-esteem	
Negotiating capability (theoretical and human)	Interpersonal relationships Forging agreements	Empathy Resourcefulness Willingness to forge agreements Positive attitude	Negotiation techniques	High self-esteem Ability to improvize	Good at public relations Good negotiator Respectful Positive attitude
Analytical ability (theoretical)	Reasoning and analysis	Analytical disposition Ability to assess cost-effectiveness	Organization Communications Strategy		Good analyst
Flexibility and self-learning (human)	New developments Change and learning	Adjusting capability		Flexibility	
Ability to commit to the organization (human)	Values moving the organization	Involvement capability		Linked to organizational values	Linked to organizational values Keeping with values
Team leadership (human)	Interaction with others	Ability for personal interactions Communications skills Resourcefulness	Team management Project management	Sound guidance	Understanding Others can learn from him/her

Table 7.1 (Continued)

Competency	Motivation: desires	Personality traits	Knowledge: know-how	Self-image	Social role
Strategic and planning capability (theoretical)	Reasoning and analysis	Ability to know where the organization is going and where it should go Ability to value alternatives' cost-effectiveness Organizational understanding	Technical knowledge on the organization and the nonprofit world Knowledge on sector environment Knowledge on corporate world		Capable individual
Capability to use IT tools (technical)			Basic software knowledge		
Capability to design projects (theoretical–technical)	Specific objectives	Strategic capability Analysis	Knowledge on project management		

Increased relational capability for governance bodies, management teams and field technicians

In a sector with numerous small- and medium-sized organizations facing increasingly common problems, collaborations with other nonprofits, as well as with public and private sector organizations, will grow significantly, as we have discussed in detail in the first part of this book. In this light, it will be more and more important for management teams and boards to be highly motivated to embark on collaborations and to have the necessary skills to negotiate and relate to other groups. Leadership based on individual charm and personalism – so typical in many nonprofits – should give way to a leadership based on capability, multidisciplinary technical knowledge, and overall sector trust and commitment, as well as a focus on improvements on living conditions for users at large. The trust of organizations' members on their respective governance bodies and management teams will be paramount for decision-making stages involving organizational transformations. In addition, empathy and a technical knowledge on public and private sector operations will also gather momentum.

Promoting collaboration projects will also force field technicians to deploy greater relational capabilities and demand all workers to fully commit to projects rather than to organizations themselves.

Decreased motivation resulting from personal achievements and enhanced teamwork skills

The new scenario will call for a massive increase in teamwork at all organizational levels. As personalistic leadership gradually fades away, organizations will increasingly need enhanced interpersonal skills and, mostly, heightened personal motivation drawn from group accomplishments and teamwork. These abilities will be most needed in technical and administrative jobs.

Increased multidisciplinary knowledge, especially for field professionals

The rising connection among social issues, as well as the increasing professionalism demands, will require greater multidisciplinary knowledge from organizations' staffs. This increase will trigger a significant change, especially among field technicians, who will have to broaden and deepen their knowledge on social intervention topics and team coordination. The new scenario focuses on a ground-breaking transformation of social work professionals' profiling. This transformation – resulting from growing demand, new social technical professions and reduced regular volunteer dedication – implies consolidated coordination and people/budget management tasks that many sector professionals already performed but that will now become instrumental. Thus, we expect a gradual evolution from an execution to a management profile and a significant shift in necessary competency types and levels.

Emergence of new, very specialized professional profiles

In addition, even if it sounds contradictory, although it is a complement of the process we have just described, gradual education and organizational adjustments to new social demands will lead to the development of a new field technician profile, with a very specialized basic knowledge and less theoretical skills than traditional social workers. We believe there will be a new profile of workers to deliver front-end services to users, who will expand massively, both quantitatively and qualitatively. These new professional profiles respond to new social demands – such as the need for occupational therapists or extra-curricular activity supervisors – or to the absorption of tasks previously carried out by outside individuals – such as housewives. In many organizations, these activities are now undertaken by social workers and volunteers, but they will certainly require a highly significant volume increase, as well as a wider range of jobs.

Increased adjustment and learning capabilities

These combined changes will inevitably demand great adjustment and learning capabilities from organizations' personnel, who will have to adapt to a faster changing environment. These capabilities depend largely on individual disposition, willingness to change and enough self-esteem to help individuals feel safe in unknown environments.

Increased information technology competencies

Despite their specificity and on account of their critical nature, we believe it is important to mention the increased technological competencies that will be necessary at almost all organizational levels.

The changes we have portrayed affect worker groups in different fashions. Table 7.2 summarizes the type of competencies that will enhance their relevance, decrease their importance or surface as new requirements for each of several worker groups.

Table 7.2	Organizational competency map		
	New	**Increased**	**Decreased**
Board	Knowledge of and empathy to other organization types and sectors – business and public spheres	Commitment to cause Strategic competency Innovation Initiative Trust-building Communications	Motivation based on personal goals
Management team	Knowledge of and empathy to other organization types and sectors – business and public spheres	Adjustment and learning Commitment to cause Strategic competency Initiative Communications	Motivation based on personal accomplishments
Administration	Innovation Co-responsibility Teamwork	Commitment to cause Adjustment and learning IT competencies	Motivation based on personal accomplishments
Field workers	Strategic competency Innovation Management knowledge IT competencies	Commitment to cause Adjustment and learning Initiative Multidisciplinary knowledge Co-responsibility Teamwork Relational capability	Motivation based on personal accomplishments
Base workers	High technical specialization	Commitment to cause Adjustment and learning Relational capability	

Having a Skillful Human Team

It seems clear that this new environment also draws a new map of necessary competencies. New capabilities emerge; others become more urgent, and a few wane in relevance. To rise to these new challenges, organizations should first assess how suited their current teams are to these demands. Do the people in the organization have the necessary competencies? After completing this analysis, the next – logical – question to ask is whether it is possible to deploy the necessary competencies with their current teams. Can these competencies be developed or strengthened accordingly? If the answer is yes, how should this process unfold?

Three notions must be clear:

1. In general, competencies may be acquired.
2. However, some competencies are easier to develop than others.
3. While the technical aspects involved in specialized knowledge are rather easy to boost, relational-oriented capabilities are more difficult to develop if they are not innate. The same applies to personality traits. Also, although they may be strengthened or weakened, subjective elements associated with self-motivation are, usually, hard to change, whereas individuals' social role is easier to mold.

These three statements lead to the conclusion that competency acquisition will depend on the elements that make up each competency. Thus, it will be possible to acquire some competencies immediately, through traditional training, while others will require more time and other tools.

In our opinion, there are four major mechanisms available to organizations to work on their human teams' competencies. As we have already mentioned, these mechanisms will have a different impact, depending on the type of competency targeted. Still, if adequately combined, these mechanisms will help organizations develop quite a complete range of competencies. These mechanisms include

1. Job design
2. Training
3. Knowledge of other situations: information exchanges, turnover, worker loan or incorporation
4. Professional career planning.

Job Design

Performing our own jobs is the best way to acquire and consolidate competencies. As most people know, experience is often the best teacher.

Yet, it should be noted that on-the-job learning processes require a good starting point, sound support and periodical thrusts. To acquire the necessary competencies to perform satisfactorily at a job, it is necessary to start by having a minimum, basic knowledge of the job, as well as the corresponding critical competencies. Organizations should bear these elements in mind for personnel recruiting and promotion.

This starting point should be supported by job descriptions based on objectives and procedures, so that individuals undertaking any specific job will know where they are expected to focus and what criteria and abilities are valued as key by their organizations. This information, which is often not supplied adequately, holds the key to ensuring that individuals' efforts to acquire competencies match organizational expectations.

The Fund-raiser

Let us revisit the example of the fund-raiser and his team. If a nonprofit organization employs a fund-raiser for the sole purpose of raising a specific revenue volume and does not explain the criteria and procedures to be used to that end, the fund-raiser may focus his competencies and try to acquire new competencies in a way that opposes the organization's ultimate goals. For example, the fund-raiser may adopt a very aggressive behavior, embracing his assignment with such personal motivation that he excludes the volunteers who used to be involved in that task. This attitude may lead him to raise the desired revenues, but it may also clash with some of the organizational values and the core competencies the organization is trying to develop in its personnel, such as teamwork and collaboration, jeopardizing its future capabilities.

Similarly significant is evaluation as articulating mechanism for competency acquisition. Evaluation allows organizations to anticipate performance problems, to know the potential of existing and necessary capabilities, and to guide volunteer and full-time workers throughout competency acquisition processes. Formal evaluations should be presented as an opportunity to learn. As pointed out by Blake, Srygley and Adams (1989), the lack of trust, sincerity, criticism and feedback may be viewed as the foremost hurdle for effective human resource utilization. Good evaluations also enable the definition of support mechanisms to be incorporated to help people or teams to develop the competencies they need. Indeed, evaluations make for very valuable information sources to formulate training plans, career plans and personnel exchange programs. Yet, the way evaluations are carried out, as well as what and who are evaluated, should match the competencies that need to be enhanced.

In an organization that wishes to promote teamwork and its corresponding capabilities, evaluations largely focusing on individual performance may be counterproductive if isolated from team evaluations. Thus, evaluations become relevant instruments to reinforce group motivation rather than individual accomplishments. Additionally, an evaluation that criticizes failed yet interesting initiatives may encourage organizational conservativeness and lack of accountability.

The need to clarify job objectives and to measure their achievement in order to ensure an effective competency acquisition process should not be associated with the existence of very restrictive job descriptions. Objectives and procedures should be set to suit the competencies that individuals are expected to develop. Thus, the more necessary the acquisition of technical or formal competencies tied to a specific job, the narrower the action framework should be. On the contrary, if initiative capabilities are important, action frameworks should be broader.

In addition, on-the-job learning is viable in most cases only if there is a person to learn from or with. Hence, working structures that feature clear supervision and capable individuals and teams including people with diverse capabilities are instrumental to boosting competency acquisition processes.

Training

Traditionally, training has been the key instrument consciously used to develop organizational competencies. However, despite its leading role, most organizations do not allocate resources to this activity. Yet, we daresay it is the most widely used mechanism to support competency acquisition, although its application has generally been limited to competencies heavily dependent on technical knowledge. This approach is closely related to the widespread notion that this kind of capabilities are the only one on which training has a direct impact. Indeed, the development of capabilities unrelated to technical knowledge is usually viewed as closely related to each job or innate and, therefore, available only through careful recruiting.

Training's core application is reflected by current educational offerings for the nonprofit sector. A hasty analysis shows that most of these offerings focus on the transmission of technical knowledge. Thus, we find numerous courses on IT training, useful practices – legal affairs, accounting and so on; functional management tools – human resources, communications; and intervention instruments – social intervention, cooperation; but there is very little education offered on relational abilities or focusing on the enhancement or development of capabilities associated with personality traits or personal attitudes. These are all key competencies for the new environment surrounding us in the present.

In line with the ideas introduced by Letts, Ryan and Grossman (1999), we could say that training offerings mainly focus on the maintenance of basic capabilities required for programs, neglecting the development of capabilities associated with the expansion, adjustment and innovation of those basic competencies. These educational offerings, as we have pointed out, revolve around a competency map that suffices for base technicians but is only necessary – and not enough – for technical workers to develop some of the new capabilities demanded of them. In addition, short seminars and technical lectures on new intervention areas may also constitute a sound instrument to strengthen multidisciplinary knowledge at virtually all organizational levels.

However, it is our belief that training should not be restricted to the acquisition of technical competencies. As some organizations are already doing, training may turn into a highly useful tool for the acquisition and strengthening of strategic competencies, skills associated with team leadership and coordination, as well as motivation, personal image building and – to a lesser extent – social roles. We refer to a form of education that is methodologically different from traditional class delivery, fostering teamwork and practical application. In this type of education, trainees are encouraged to draw personal conclusions from shared starting points that favor reflection and attitude transformation – motivation and self-esteem. It also intends to promote specific personality traits and abilities and to curb others.

Such is the case, for example, of practical seminars on management skills, or on personal work to discover and strengthen individual skills. These courses help attendants to acquire some of the capabilities required to act as managers – skills that many field workers are going to need in the new scenario. We are also referring to communications, self-knowledge and managerial style seminars, which nonprofits' governance body and management team members will need more than ever before.

We believe internal training processes, combining seminars, workshops and meetings, will enable organizations to analyze their environments and to develop organizational diagnoses that will help their members to join in strategic decisions, fueling their commitment and prompting the need to adjust and innovate within the framework of organizational values. In this case, we refer to integrated training, embedded in organizations' dynamics, which turns into a wonderful tool to strengthen members' competencies and to convey the need for change.

In our opinion, training's potential to develop capabilities is clearly underexploited. Every organization should explore and enhance this potential, both internally and through outside resource offerings. Mapping existent and desirable competencies provides a good starting point to design more or less ambitious training plans to gradually build organizations' desired competency scheme. In this regard, the entire sector faces the challenge of surveying their educational demands and streamlining them in such a way that generic offerings match their current needs. This improvement will have a direct impact on smaller organizations' possibilities to adjust their existing competencies. Generic outside offerings should not completely substitute for internal training, but they should allow organizations to focus their training on commitment strengthening and specific ability development.

The Environmental Organization and Its Training Plan

After a careful strategic analysis, the board of an environmental organization establishes its strategic need to broaden its operations from specific intervention activities – waste collection, beach cleaning – to a more proactive advocacy involvement. To that end, the organization needs to reach internal consensus and to change its members' competencies. In order to focus on these goals, the organization formulates a one-year training plan including the following:

- courses on theoretical information regarding current major environmental issues.
- monthly debates on the links between those challenges and public administration actions in each of the communities where the organization is based.
- workshops for multidisciplinary teams – involving all organizational levels – to anticipate and discuss future challenges.

Knowledge of Other Situations: Information Exchanges, Turnover, Worker Loan or Incorporation

One of the easiest ways to learn is to get to know how others act. By looking around and having the opportunity to share and to analyze how other teams or organizations work, organizations seize a key mechanism to enable their human teams to access new technical knowledge and to break away from the assumption that things should always be done in a certain way, opening up new paths and promoting the desire and the ability to change. Although, obviously, organizations should not necessarily use and apply everything they see and they learn, getting to know other realities fosters the development of some competencies.

This knowledge may be brought about by simply promoting exchanges through cross-organization coordination activities, debate or training forums, or even through sector websites. However, it may be taken to a higher level by undertaking joint or exchange projects, loaning or incorporating members from other teams or organizations. For instance, the creation of sector associations and the promotion of training and exchange options through second-tier organizations may provide a means to enhance overall sector competencies.

These mechanisms imply different commitments and costs for organizations, but they should be considered for specific circumstances, depending on how critical and suitable competencies are in any given situation. Thus, for example, it is important for team members to recognize that undertaking shared projects and truly interacting with other organizations' personnel often constitute not only field-related needs but also great opportunities to develop specific competencies. Indeed, organizations should determine who will be involved in a project not only on the basis of disposition, but also according to individuals' capabilities and needs to acquire specific competencies. As a matter of fact, these decisions should also contemplate individuals' career planning potential within their organizations. Working with other teams or in other organizational environments, individuals are offered an opportunity to change their social role and their own perceptions of themselves. It also allows them to unearth previously undetected competencies. The possibility to acquire new competencies by discovering other realities and the experience provided by working with people from other organizations should also be factored in the design of training plans.

A helpful mechanism to ensure organization members acquire the competencies that their jobs or organizations cannot provide for them lies in personnel exchanges. Yet, this is one of the most complex processes to embark on, be it through inner mobility within the organization – what is usually referred to as internal turnover or transfer – or through exchanging, loaning or incorporating people from other organizations.

Internal turnover affords the chance to discover other realities, to perform new tasks and to break away from routine. It may be used to enhance individuals' adjustment capabilities and to develop new competencies for transferring individuals and the teams that receive them. Turnover fosters role changing in teams and leads to the introduction of new ideas, knowledge and competencies, which may clearly influence origin and, mostly, destination teams. Indeed, internal turnover experiences constitute a very useful tool to work on both individual and team competencies. However, it is far from easy. There are obvious costs involved as a result of temporary adjustments and efficiency losses and the need to negotiate with team heads, who do not necessarily understand the potential benefit of switching or loaning an already trained individual. If inadequately communicated or carried out, it may even cause harmful misunderstandings among collaborators.

If internal turnover is complex, personnel exchanges and loans between organizations may seem downright illusory. Nevertheless, we daresay that nonprofits are probably the best type of organizations to experiment with this tool to strengthen their team competencies. Incorporating people from other organizations is not at all infrequent in organizations that generally feature a significant number of volunteer workers. Volunteer work provides a highly relevant source of organizational renewal and incorporation of new competencies. We are referring to not only the competencies volunteers have but also those they can transmit. Volunteer workers bring their technical knowledge from other sectors or organizations; they have experienced other working habits, other organizational cultures that may be extremely useful for the teams they join. Organizations should learn to explore the potential of their volunteers beyond the specific jobs they have joined for.

Professional Career Planning

It seems clear that job performance entails a great opportunity to develop competencies. However, we all know that, after some time, the learning curve drops sharply. This fall is even more pronounced in the acquisition of competencies associated with social role, motivation and relational capability.

The downward turn of learning curves should be borne in mind, since it may hinder the acquisition of necessary competencies and undermine workers' motivation. Jobs should be designed to include clearly defined yet open objectives and procedures to allow workers to gradually take on new responsibilities and action fields. This is a key factor to prevent increasing routine. Still, as we have seen, this is not always possible, or desirable: it depends on existing workers' capabilities and those they are expected to acquire.

The possibility to broaden responsibilities or to transfer individuals within an organization should be a key component in organizational career planning.

A Possible Career Path for a Field Technician in Drug Addiction

- Background: college education + specialization in drug addiction.
- Minimum six-month working experience.
- Incorporation as deputy field technician.
- No direct management responsibility over volunteer teams for six months.
- On-site volunteer management training.
- Working with volunteers.
- Responsibility over a volunteer team: one year.
- Budgetary training.

We are not referring to career planning as the only means to ensure organizational growth, nor do we endorse individual career plans. We refer to forecasting and briefly designing the growth potential offered by the organization to each job profile – if that should be the case; for some jobs this will not be feasible or desirable. Organizations should map the necessary competencies for professional growth, establishing the mechanisms required to drive that acquisition. These mechanisms include training, internal turnover, experience exchanges and knowledge updating. Mapping the path field workers should follow in their jobs or until they reach a service coordinator position, indicating the specific competencies required in each stage, enables people to work individually and collectively to develop an organizational profile that leads to greater impact.

Sometimes, planning certain professional careers – mostly in top management levels, but increasingly so, as well, in field work coordination areas – requires prior experience in other organizations and sectors. This practical knowledge favors individuals' disposition toward collaboration, strengthens their empathy capabilities and ensures their familiarity with other organizations and sectors – a knowledge that is hard to acquire through other mechanisms. From this outlook, the increasing need to promote sector-wide and cross-sector professional career becomes more evident. Indeed, this process is currently supported by increasing efforts to use new technologies to publish nonprofits volunteer and full-time job openings.

The Influence of Organizational Structure and Culture

The success and impact of these activities will, to a large extent, ride on the context in which they are undertaken: the organizational structure and culture (the set of values, beliefs and principles that, explicitly and implicitly, guide the behavior of organization members). We should not forget, as Boyatzis pointed out (1982), that performance hinges not only on having certain competencies but also on the organizational environment that surrounds them. And not just that: a sound organizational structure may enhance or hinder specific competencies. From this perspective, it is important that the desired competency map and the acquisition mechanisms used to secure those competencies take into account organizations' existing structures. Organizational structures will determine critical competencies – as we have seen, a hierarchical structure will require less initiative capabilities than other organizational structures – and, at the same time, will provide the framework for the development of collaborators' competencies. Knowing the kind of structure an organization has will help determine which competencies will be required, which will be acquired easily and which will call for external support. Additionally, the analysis of the overall competencies required for organizational survival or success may reveal the need to change an organizational structure that does not favor the acquisition of such competencies.

Generally speaking, flat organizations based on teamwork tend to promote initiative and relational capabilities, but often hinder the acquisition of more specific, technical competencies. Thus, they need more skilled individuals to promote their growth and contribute value to the organization. Hierarchical structures or teams featuring a clearly defined leadership usually provide the necessary grounds to foster and strengthen technical and knowledge-related capabilities. Authoritarian, highly personalistic management styles also boost technical learning, but tend to restrict initiative and hamper the development of relational skills. At the same time, project-based organizational structures, where field and management workers work together, drive all collaborators to share an overall knowledge of entire processes, promoting the acquisition of conceptual capabilities. This approach reinforces workers' commitment to organizational causes, but it may weaken their commitment to the organization itself – which is usually stronger in centralized organizations.

In addition to the elements we have already mentioned, organizational structure and culture greatly shape the acquisition process of competencies associated with individuals' social role, self-image and motivation. For example, it is interesting to watch how the value granted by an organization to its volunteer and full-time personnel, both in its formal statements as well as in its responsibility assignments, determines the social role of people in both groups and their respective competencies. Organizations may enhance volunteers' initiative development and strengthen their ability to share project and cause responsibilities by explicitly acknowledging the role played by volunteers as a link to society. This strengthening will result both from the greater value – social role – granted by the organization and their co-workers to volunteers as well as their self-image improvements.

In addition, the existence of adequate communication formulas and involvement structures, that ensure organizational members' confidence in governance bodies, will boost their social role as organization's leaders and representatives, enhancing their competency to make strategic decisions. This competency, in turn, will favor the development of a participative culture within the organization.

Organizational culture also determines the promotion or hindering of specific competencies. A culture based on collaboration will encourage this type of work and strengthen negotiating and relational capabilities. On the contrary, an organizational culture stemming from a confrontational or critical approach – not at all infrequent in this sector – will largely hamper empathy and cross-sector knowledge development. An organization featuring a participative culture will foster the acquisition of competencies associated with new ideas and initiatives, while it will also strengthen workers' social roles as potential idea contributors and project designers.

Conclusions

Sector setting, organizational structure, individual competencies and job description build the key fabric that shapes organizational performance – in which organizations themselves hold a clear responsibility and which may be enhanced significantly by competency work.

Thus, we may safely say that building and setting in place the necessary mechanisms to ensure people's skills is crucial to consolidate organizations and to strengthen the nonprofit sector. This strength will, in turn, buttress every organization in the sector, prodding the acquisition of competencies by both volunteer and full-time workers. The ultimate goal for this acquisition is none other than a better use of nonprofits' resources to enhance the sector's overall impact.

CHAPTER 8

Final Considerations

We began this book by describing how much progress has been made over the past few years to improve nonprofit organizations' management. As we mentioned in the first chapter, it is safe to say that, in general terms, the nonprofit sector has left behind the "goodwill" culture, based on "doing good", that characterized it for a number of years, to move on to a new working philosophy that embraces the notion of "doing good well". This mindset change implies a significant qualitative leap that greatly contributes to the definite development and strengthening of the third sector as the true "third pillar" in our democratic society.

Indeed, even optimistically surveying the reality of a moving, developing third sector, we must admit that, so far, most improvements have largely focused on organizations' internal management aspects – that is, third-sector organizations have made significant progress in professionally planning and pursuing strategies and functional development to ensure greater effectiveness and efficiency.

In the current transitional stage toward a relational society, additionally seasoned by the trends we have tried to summarize in our introductory chapter as the pressures affecting nonprofits, to the extent, even, of posing dilemmas that involve the very heart of their values, this professionalization does not, however, suffice to guarantee third-sector organizations' success and adjustment to new scenarios and social demands (Table 8.1). What is more important, that professionalization is not enough to ensure that nonprofits will be capable of building trust.

There is still a long way to go, and the urgent challenges faced by the nonprofit sector no longer revolve around organizations' internal management or in areas such as communications, funding, strategic planning or human resources, but, rather, they focus on aspects such as collaboration, transparency, accountability, governance and innovation capabilities. All these aspects refer to capacity building, which we have defined as the third phase in organizational development, after value and mission setting and the commitment to ongoing learning and improvements – as shown in the figure we present once again (Figure 8.1). This is, precisely, the focal point of this book.

The message we have tried to convey throughout this book focuses on the urgent need for nonprofit organizations to strengthen, jointly with their

Table 8.1	Tensions affecting nonprofits
Competition	Collaboration
Communication	Mission
One-time involvement	Long-term involvement
Advocacy action	Service provision
Short-term charity	Long-term development
Particularism	Universalism
Continuity	Innovation

Source: Elaborated by the authors.

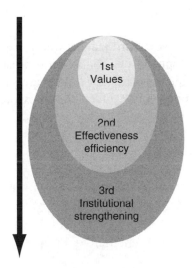

1st stage: Mission and value development

2nd stage: Commitment to ongoing improvement and learning

3rd stage: Development of competences for collaboration, trust-building and innovation

Figure 8.1 Capacity building stages. *Source*: Elaborated by the authors

stakeholders, organizational and sectorial staff, in order to face current environmental changes and to continue contributing to improve the living conditions of the people and communities they support, while maintaining and enhancing the trust society has placed in them. Only a cohesive, collaborating, transparent, innovating and "value-governed" nonprofit sector will be able to consolidate the place conquered by organizations and to become a true participant – along with the public and private for-profit sectors – of the relational society that is rapidly setting in.

In any case, it should be noted that the stages we have outlined must be viewed not as isolated and discretional but, rather, as layers to be added as organizations go forward in their road to capacity building. In other words, the theoretical model introduced is an additive construct – its center holding values at all times, as shown in Figure 8.2.

When we turn our attention to organizational efficiency and effectiveness, we cannot leave values behind; on the contrary, since efficiency and effectiveness improvements oftentimes strain organizational values. Similarly, as we move toward capacity building, we should not neglect the previous stages. In short, the model we advocate includes an initial stage, in which a focus on values is usually critical, followed by a broadened focus that incorporates managerial issues to enhance efficiency and effectiveness. Finally, as the organization moves on and finds it necessary to enlarge its impact capability, it will have to incorporate capacity building to its focus.

Few organizations are fully immersed in their third stage as described here – that is, the stage involving the development of collaboration, trust-building and innovation capabilities. The question is, why? Why are not there more institutionally strengthened nonprofits? Over the previous

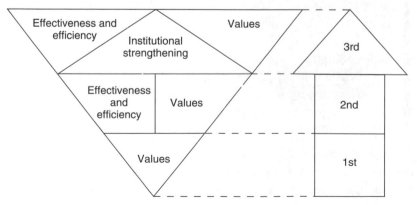

Figure 8.2 Capacity building stages. *Source*: Elaborated by the authors

pages, we have tried to offer some tips to move in that direction. Now, to conclude, we would like to name a few of the barriers that hinder capacity building. We shall refer to the three levels discussed in this book: people, organizations and sector.

Personal Barriers for Capacity Building

When we refer to nonprofit organizations, we bump into a recurrent theme that is very hard to tackle in a management book: "personal agendas". A volunteer organization usually stems from the determination of several people who come together to improve living conditions in a specific area or for a specific population group. These social entrepreneurs – sometimes, two people and, often, more – devote a lot of time and effort to develop the idea and to build the organization. Gradually, if they do it well, have a little luck and their cause is worthy, the organization starts growing. For the initial group of entrepreneurs, the organization is like an offspring, a very precious creation.

Then, if this nonprofit is successful, it will have to "release" some of its members, so that they may work, in exchange for a salary, for the organization's cause. Over a few years, the organization has undergone many transformations, has grown and outgrown its founders' original idea. However, at this point, some organizational members – its founders or other people who have become too involved with the organization's cause – occasionally prioritize their personal agendas to that of the organization. In other words, they confuse the organization's mission with their own desires and aspirations.

Organizations should try to break free from specific individuals. Indeed, Argyris and Schön (1978) explain that organizations are more than just a group of individuals, although organizations would not exist without those groups – organizations are more than the sum of individuals. Therefore, organizations should depend on all their individuals, but not on any one of them in particular, for, otherwise, they would not fulfill their organizational potential. To put it simply, people working in nonprofits should leave their own personal agendas at the door – to pick them up on their way out.

As we mentioned in the first chapter, Ulrich Beck (2002) refers to this phenomenon from a different – also interesting and contemporary – outlook. He talks about "altruistic individualism" or "collaborating selfishness" to explain that many youngsters collaborate with the third sector to "personally experience how to choose individualism and social morality again, and how to interrelate free will and individualism with living for others".

Specifically, Beck relies on the studies undertaken by US sociologist Robert Wuthnow, whose findings – in Beck's opinion and ours, as well – may also be applicable to Europe and other Western areas. Beck writes (2002: 73), "[…Wuthnow] draws the interesting conclusion that young adults, who embody the most decisive selfish values, focusing on their careers and self-satisfaction, etc., are, at the same time, the ones who highly value community activities and devote a large portion of their free time to others." He also adds, "I find this paradox to be extremely interesting, […] highly appreciating selfishness and showing a strong disposition to help others."

Naturally, this notion of "collaborating selfishness" bears many implications for nonprofits gazing at the future. Beck believes "this is hard to understand for social aid institutions: many people are no longer willing to act as lowly troopers in the hierarchical administration of social aid".

Along with "personal agendas", surely the most significant barrier for capacity building at human level relates to leadership. Oddly enough, this is one of the topics that has commanded more attention in management bibliography and that has shown the greatest development.[1] Gardner (1990) puts this notion in very suitable terms for our purpose, "some leaders are, perhaps, very talented to solve problems personally, but if they fail when it comes to institutionalizing this process, their departure severely weakens the organizations they leave behind".

Several people have written extensively on leadership over the years, first referring to the business world and, later, focusing on the nonprofit sector. Doubtlessly, Peter Drucker is one of the authors who have made significant contributions in this field. Drucker (1996) highlights the notion of "missionary leaders". In his own words, "the only definition that suits a leader is someone who has followers", and he adds, "a person who gets results, sets an example and takes responsibility".

Although this is not a book on leadership, we would like to point out that instances in which leaders have been praised to a mythical level are not the most suitable for twenty-first-century third-sector organizations.

Some contributions on this topic are especially interesting for this book, for they emphasize the relational aspects of leadership. For example, Mary Tschirhart (1996) has stressed how important it is for leaders to manage organizational contact networks. Drath and Palus (1994) view leadership as "a process that takes place in a certain context, unfolding through time". These two authors also uphold a more community-oriented notion of leadership, adding that, in this kind of leadership process, "the entire community is involved".

Thus, leadership is not restricted to a series of actions carried out by individuals bearing specific characteristics. Rather, it is a process in which individuals jointly develop a vision of what the world (or a portion of it) should be like and interpret reality in a similar fashion. Therefore, leadership creation is always a collective process (Ospina, Godsoe and Schall, 2002).

Drath and Palus (2002) view leadership as the creation of meaning in a community (organization, in this case). Leadership is the result of a joint process of meaning generation undertaken by people – and not the opposite (a leader creates leadership, which, in turn, creates a collective organizational vision). A person with formal or informal authority is just one more participant – more powerful than others, though – in the leadership process, and leadership is not restricted exclusively to that person. This notion of leadership may be useful to our purposes. The people who intend to strengthen their organizations and to overcome personal barriers hindering capacity building should regard leadership as a collective process that creates common meaning and understanding frameworks.

Organizational Barriers for Capacity Building

Organizational hurdles vary in nature (McKinsey and Company, 2001). First, organizations tend to prioritize "social aid" and, hence, programs and projects having outside impact, neglecting initiatives that focus on strengthening organizational competencies. This attitude – in most cases, the result of the entrepreneurial capability of the people in nonprofit organizations – is usually known as "programmatic vision". Some organizations' cultures tend to appreciate their work in priority projects and programs more than the tasks involved in organizational management and administration.

In addition, for many organizations, especially small ones, capacity building may turn into a difficult and costly endeavor, particularly on a short-term basis. Usually, leaders in these organizations prefer to focus their few resources on programs bearing a direct outside impact.

Second, organizations experience a damaging shortage of knowledge on capacity building. In areas such as fund-raising or quality service, organizations may resort to existing bibliography, sector consultants or past experiences drawn from similar organizations. Instead, in the field of capacity building, taking into account the features we mentioned in our introduction (no magic formulas; the need to adjust to local conditions; the process notion; the necessary involvement of beneficiaries; working on the three levels – individuals, organization and sector, etc.), there is no single benchmark or approach that suits all organizations.

Third, there is no favorable environment for capacity building. Most donors, especially public administrations and specialized agencies, provide the funds for projects and programs having a visible outside impact, in which only a small share is used to support organizational overhead. In the sphere of international cooperation, for example, while past nonprofits funding models could be described as "blank checks", current relationships between donors and nonprofits are ruled by strict service delivery and subsidy contracts – sometimes granted through public bidding – that include strict expense controls. The recent emergence, mainly in the Anglo-Saxon world, and in Europe as well, of institutions – mostly foundations – devoted to third-sector capacity building contributes to overcoming this obstacle.

Indeed, what we advocate here is the need to develop learning organizations (Senge, 1990) that can enhance organizational learning, both internally and in their environments (Argyris and Schon, 1978). Then, the question now is, when are organizations able to learn? According to Argyris and Schon (1978), organizations learn when their members are able to respond to inner and outer situations with solutions, and these solutions become a part of organizational procedures, thus overcoming internal and external barriers. In addition, Senge (1990) states that learning is possible when individuals know themselves and share mental models, and when organizations share a common vision and are able to work in teams.

Sector Barriers for Capacity Building

Linked to the last hurdle we mentioned in the previous section, the sector itself may hinder individual organizations' capacity building. A nonprofit sector lacking a minimum self-regulatory and self-governance capability may fall prey to vicious cycles that would lead the entire sector to a harmful shortsightedness that only lets it see everyday operations. The increasing competition for resources – which is not necessarily negative in itself – combined with an overall inability to set a minimum standard for joint action may drive the sector down a negative spiral, focusing more and more on daily operations and neglecting capacity building. To offset these situations, the third sector needs to build formal and informal ties among organizations and to establish the rules of the game, setting acceptable standards. Indeed, we believe people and organizations should create a minimum social capital to overcome sector barriers.

However, the relationship between capacity building, organizational impact and social capital has turned out to be quite elusive. In some cases, the connection may be straightforward. For example, in a food bank, it is clear that stock management improvements lead to food distribution enhancements and greater impact in terms of services to beneficiaries. In the case of relief organizations, an improvement in information systems to handle collaborations with other organizations, added to the development of food safety measurements, for instance, could directly increase organizational and sector capabilities to respond to natural disasters. Nevertheless, in most cases, these connections are not so straightforward, and it is very hard to isolate the benefits of capacity building initiatives from other outside – legal, economic, political or social – factors.

The Notion of Social Capital

There are several definitions of *social capital*, a concept increasingly used, not only in academic circles, but also in the realm of public policy, especially in the field of sustainable development. The World Bank defines it as "the institutions, relations and norms that ultimately define the quantity and quality of social interactions". According to the World Bank, experience has proven that social cohesion constitutes a critical factor for sustainable development. And, according to the same organization, social capital refers not only to the sum of institutions underlying a specific society, but also to the "glue" that holds these institutions together. For the OECD, social capital is defined as "the networks and shared norms, values and understandings that promote cooperation at the heart of social groups and among them".

In most cases, the term refers to "a social resource for collective action", that is created and accumulated through the formal and informal relationships built among the people in any given community. The term *social capital* describes, essentially, the social environment where people live, and it constitutes a collective resource available to them, their families and their communities.

A few worthy annotations on this notion include:

- It is not an accurate concept, and several current debates still focus on its meaning.
- However, within the field of Social Sciences, definitions seem to agree on the emphasis on networks and civil norms. In general, the notion of social capital refers to the internal social and cultural coherence found in any society, to the norms and values that rule interactions between people and existing institutions.
- The concept of social capital is very helpful to understand how cohesive a community is, and it may contribute useful ideas to read into social and economic characteristic variations.
- Social capital may be accrued when people interact with other families, in neighborhoods, in organizations and in other formal and informal meeting venues.

However, not all experts seem to agree on this outlook. Some, like Putnam (2000), Backman and Smith (2000), Cernea (1994) or Boris (1999), uphold that engagement in formal and informal organizations is a key factor to build the confidence of people and institutions and to promote specific social interaction behaviors. By gathering people, nonprofit organizations mobilize individuals to collective action, providing them with a chance to "be heard" in public circles. Indeed, organizations' capacity building is a key to building social capital. As Cernea (1994: 9) states, nonprofits "promote trust and social interaction by defining members' mutual obligations and rights, by creating roles and specialized tasks in organizations, by setting internal authority and accountability systems, by fostering standards and behaviors viewed as useful and collectively relevant, and by precluding those that are perceived as detrimental". In other words, nonprofit organizations account for a suitable framework for people to interact and to work together to accomplish shared goals, usually of common interest.

Although it is true that the relationship between capacity building per se and social capital is not always easy to pinpoint, since many other factors should be taken into account, undoubtedly many nonprofits – especially those devoted to public welfare and collective interest – contribute to build and strengthen the bonds among people and to create a community "infrastructure" through phenomena such as volunteer work, social interaction among organization members and community users or beneficiaries, or connections between board members and communities (De Vita and Fleming, 2001). Thus, if capacity building may help – and it does – nonprofits to pursue their missions more effectively and to perform the role assigned to them by the new model outlined in society, it is a key factor, also, for the construction and development of social capital, even if the connection is indirect and impossible to prove scientifically.

Social Innovators, Social Learning Organizations and a Mediating Capital Nonprofit Sector

First, we would like to stress the fact that the capacity building hurdles we have mentioned in the previous section are far from insurmountable. Recent trends, such as the growing professionalization of nonprofit organizations and leaders, coupled with the positive capacity building experiences collected by some organizations and the emergence of increasingly favorable funding conditions for such initiatives and projects, may act as powerful forces to assist in the creation of a new organizational culture and a deep commitment to capacity building.

There is, however, a prerequisite to drive this qualitative change within nonprofits and their entire sector. This prerequisite is the leadership ability of nonprofits' workers, especially those at management and governance levels. In short, beyond strategies, policies, systems and procedures, it is all about people. Often, it is effective leadership that makes the difference between success and failure when policies, programs and services are carried out.

Organizations do not only need leaders who are committed to their organizational missions, who have a vision and are able to pour organizational ideals into strategies. In the new environment setting, nonprofits need leaders who are committed to organizational "excellence", "flexibility", "innovation" and "vitality", who are able to understand community needs and the role played by their organizations, who can think creatively, strengthen their organizations' image, prestige and reputation. Finally, organizational leaders need to relate to other social agents, building collaborations and forging agreements. To sum up, today nonprofits need "innovating leaders or social entrepreneurs".

Second, as we bring this book to an end, we would like to highlight another of its focal points: the need for nonprofits to be socially intelligent. Socially intelligent organizations work on long-term goals, building collaborations with other – private and public – organizations in order to seek solutions to the new challenges faced by society. Socially intelligent organizations have incorporated their role in relational society and do not only look for their own benefits, but try to enhance the social impact of their operations.

Nonprofit organizations will secure their legitimacy when their social impact is clearly understood by society at large. In other words, third-sector organizations that focus on their own "survival" and try to stay afloat simply as another player in the economic whole, neglecting to work to transform society and to bear a significant social impact, will end up losing their legitimacy.

Working to bear a significant social impact means realizing that organizations cannot operate on their own. Thus, we insist on the notion of socially intelligent, relationally intelligent organizations. Nonprofits must find new solutions to old social problems, while they seek new solutions to new social challenges. Developing their capabilities for ongoing innovation and learning will be instrumental to reducing these tensions.

At the same time, most social nonprofits work to support very specific and worthy causes, such as helping Down-syndrome afflicted people, promoting new technologies for adult women, improving education for teenagers in large cities through leisure activities and so on. Nonprofits' specificity is the key to their success – it is necessary, and it shows civil society's innovating abilities. Still, in a plural and multicultural society, excessive specificity may lead to social problems. We need social organizations to fight specific ills, but to embrace universal values. In this issue, it is crucial to avoid the false local-versus-global dichotomy. Every global organization has local roots.[2]

In finding consensus on universal values, social organizations face an enormous challenge and must mitigate the existing tension in society. John Gray (2000) suggests that we should try to respond pragmatically to the cultural pluralism looming over us, since we are unable to reach universal consensus on values. Gray's proposal rides on the possibility to build social balance on the acknowledgement of conflicting rights, which may be sorted out through peaceful agreements. More important, many nonprofits are already doing just that.

In short, the key for nonprofits to become institutionally stronger lies in socially innovating people, socially intelligent organizations and a sector that builds mediating capital.

Notes

1 Introduction

1. In this book, we will refer to nonprofit organizations using this term or its synonymous expressions: civil society organizations, third-sector organizations, social organizations, volunteer organizations and/or non-governmental organizations.
2. See M. Lindenberg and C. Bryant, 2001.
3. In this book, the term "welfare State" is used broadly to refer to all Western democracies, indiscriminately engulfing all Anglo-Saxon, Southern European or Northern European models.
4. In view of the demographic evolution of Western nations it is not possible that a single actor will have the capacity of providing care to the elderly on its own.
5. Harvard Business School Professor Martha Minow (2002) explores this dichotomy in her book *Partners, Not Rivals: Privatization and the Public Good*.
6. See P. Light (2004).
7. See Minkoff (2002).
8. See, for example, the excellent book by J. Austin et al., *Social Partnering in Latin America* (2004)

Part 1 Collaboration

1. We will not analyze business–government relations, since this book focuses on nonprofit organizations.

2 Collaborations Between Businesses and Nonprofits: Approaching Corporate Citizenship

1. This program is currently underway (Salerno, 2001, private communication).
2. Companies that use the "matching funds" method donate the same total amount of money contributed by their employees to a specific cause, thus doubling the overall donation received by the beneficiary organization.
3. "The NGO–industrial complex." Gary Gereffi, Ronie Garcia-Johnson, Erika Sasser. *Foreign Policy*. Washington: Jul/Aug 2001, Iss. 125, p. 56.

3 Collaborations Between Public Administrations and Nonprofits: Towards a Relational Society

1. Bresser Pereira, Luiz Carlos; Cunill Grau, Nuria. 1998. Lo Publico No Estatal En La Reforma Del Estado. Paidós, Buenos Aires.
2. Lester M. Salamon and Helmut K. Anheier. 1998. *Social Origins of Civil Society: Explaining the* Nonprofit Sector Cross-Nationally. Voluntas: *International Journal of Voluntary and Nonprofit Organizations.* Volume 9, Number 3, pp. 213–48.
3. We shall revisit this topic when we discuss collaborations among nonprofit organizations.
4. Ultimately, in most cases, public–private collaborations materialize through contracts, agreements or subsidies.

4 Collaborations Among Nonprofits: An Immediate Challenge

1. M. Lindenberg and J. P. Dobel, 1999. The Challenges of Globalization for Northern International Relief and Development NGOs. *Nonprofit and Voluntary Sector Quarterly.* Vol. 28, Iss. 4, p. 4.
2. Table 4.3 is inspired on the guidelines suggested by A. Turovh Himmelman, in Huxman (1996).

Part II   Competencies Required for Third-Sector Capacity Building

1. Readers may wonder why we have not inverted these two parts, then. We have preferred to talk first about collaborations and relational society to encourage nonprofit organizations to embark on the capability strengthening process we explain in the second part. To strengthen these competencies calls for a significant effort from most third-sector organizations, although we truly believe results will be worth it.

5 Accountability Elements in Nonprofits

1. It is not the purpose of this chapter to discuss the recent instances in which business companies and public organizations have escaped the market and public administration control mechanisms.

6 Nonprofits' Governance Bodies and Governability

1. This happens in private business boards as well.
2. However, this does not mean that renewal is a guarantee in itself. Organizations need to be committed to "improve what they already have".

3. Yet, we should temper this statement by admitting that the incorporation of people to several boards provides organizations with vast overall sector knowledge and a profound commitment to "relational" principles.
4. Both quotes have been taken from an excellent article by John Carver (2001) on board management – specifically from a section that intends to justify the role of boards as governors.

8 Final Considerations

1. See, for instance, *The Leader of the Future: New Visions, Strategies, and Practices for the Next Era*. San Francisco, CA, Jossey-Bass, 1996.
2. Beck (2000) uses the term "glocal".

BIBLIOGRAPHY

Annan, Kofi. 2000. "The Global Compact". www.unglobalcompact.org.

Argyris, Chris, and Donald A. Schön. 1978. *Organizational Learning: A Theory of Action Perspective*. Reading: Addison-Wesley.

Arsenault, J. 1998. *Forging Nonprofit Alliances: A Comprehensive Guide to Enhancing Your Mission Through Joint Ventures & Partnerships, Management Service Organisations, Parent Corporations and Mergers*. San Francisco: Jossey-Bass.

Austin, David M., and Yeheskel Hasenfeld. 1985. A Prefatory Essay on the Future Administration of Human Services. *The Journal of Applied Behavioral Science*, 21, no. 4: 351–64.

Austin, James. 2000. Principles for Partnership. *Leader to Leader*, no. 18.

——. 2001a. Connecting with Nonprofits. *HBS Working Knowledge*.

——. 2001b. Entering the Age of Alliance. *HBS Working Knowledge*.

Austin, James *et al.* 2004. Social Partnering in Latin America. Cambridge: Harvard University Press.

Backman, E., and S. Smith. 2000. Healthy Organisation, Unhealthy Communities. *Nonprofit Management and Leadership*, 10, no. 4: 355–73.

Bardach, Eugene. 1998. *Getting Agencies to Work Together. The Practice and Theory of Managerial Craftsmanship*. Washungton: Brookings Institution Press.

Beck, Ulrich. 2000. *What is Globalization?* Oxford: Blackwell.

——. 2002. *Libertad o Capitalismo*. Barcelona: Paidos Estado y Sociedad.

Belil, Mireia, Vernis, Alfred. 1996. *La excelencia en el sector no lucrativo. Una comparación regional*. Comisión de las Comunidades Europeas. Dirección General XXIII/A/4. Barcelona: Dossiers Barcelona Associacions 24.

Berger, Gabriel, and Poli, María. 2000. *Manual para el Fortalecimiento de Consejos Directivos de Organizaciones Sin Fines de Lucro*. Buenos Aires: Foro del Sector Social.

Berger, Hans, Niels Noorderhaven, Bart Nooteboom, and Bartjan Pennink. 1993. Understanding the Subcontracting Relationship: The Limitations of Transaction Cost Economics. *Societal Change Between Market and Organization*, ed. John Child, Michel Crozier, Renate Mayntz, *et al.* Aldershot (England): Avebury.

Berger, Peter, and Richard Neuhaus. 1977. *To Empower People*. Washington, DC: American Enterprise Institute for Public Policy Research.

Blake, R., J. Srygley, and A. Adams. 1989. *Change by Design*. Massachusetts: Wesley Publishing.

Bolger, J. 2000. Capacity Development: Why, What and How. *CIDA Policy Branch Occasional Series* I, no. I.

Boris, E. 1999. The Nonprofit Sector in the 1990s. *En Philantropy and the Nonprofit Sector*, ed. Charles T. Clotfelter, and Thomas Ehrlich. Bloomington, Indiana University Press.

Bossuyt, J. 1994. Capacity Development: How can Donors do it Better? *ECPDM Policy Management Brief*, no. 5.

Boyatzis, Richard E. 1982. *The Competent Manager: A Theory of Effective Performance*. New York, NY John Wiley & Sons.

Bresser, Luíz Carlos. 1997. Reforma del Estado en los años 90: Lógica y Mecanismos de Control. Barcelona: Círculo de Montevideo.

Bresser Pereira, L. C., and Cunill, N. 1998. *Lo público no estatal en la reforma del Estado*, Buenos Aires: Paidos.

Brinkerhoff, Derick W. 1995. Technical Cooperation for Capacity-Building in Strategic Policy Management in Developing Countries. 56th Conference of the American Society for Public AdministrationSan Antonio: US Agency for International Development.

Carver, John. 1997. *Boards that Make a Difference*. San Francisco: Jossey-Bass.

———. 2001. *John Carver on Board Leadership: Selected Writings from the Creator of the World's Most Provocative and Systematic Governance Model*. San Francisco: Jossey-Bass.

Castiñeira, Angel, and Vidal, Pau. 2003. *Llibre Blanc del Tercer Sector Cívic-Social*. Barcelona: Observatori del Tercer Sector.

Cattacin, Sandro. 1996. Organiser les solidarités: La construction du bien-être par l'interface public-privé en Europe. *Crise et recomposition des solidarités. Vers un nouvel équilibre Etat – société civile*. Marc-Henry Soulet. Universitaires de Fribourg. 313.

Centre d'Estudis de Temes Contemporaniis. 2002. *Llibre blanc del tercer sector civico-social*. Barcelona: Centre d'Estudis de Temes Contemporaniis.

Cernea, M. 1994. The Sociologist's Approach to Sustainable Development. Making Development Sustainable: from Concepts to Action. *Environmentally Sustainable Development Occasional Paper (Series Ns 2)*. Serageldin, Ismail; Steer; Andrew Washington, DC: The World Bank.

Christine W. Letts, William P. Ryan, and Allen Grossman. 1999. *High Performance Nonprofit Organizations: Managing Upstream for Greater Impact*. New York, Wiley & Sons.

Charities Aid Foundation, CAF. 1998. *Benchmarking Charity Costs*. Glasgow: GreenGate Publishing.

Comisión Europea. 2001. *Libro Verde; Fomentar un marco europeo para la responsabilidad de las empresas*. Bruselas: Comision Europea.

Debra C. Minkoff. 2002. The Emergence of Hybrid Organizational Forms: Combining Identity-Based Service Provision and Political Action. *Nonprofit and Voluntary Sector Quarterly*, 31: 377–401

De Vita, J., and C. Fleming. 2001. *Building Capacity in Nonprofit Organizations*. Washington DC: The Urban Institute.

Drath, Wilfred H., and Charles J. Palus. 1994. *Making Common Sense: Leadership as Meaning-Making in a Community of Practice*. Washington: CCL Press.

Drucker, Peter. 1999. La información que los directivos necesitan realmente. *Cómo medir el rendimiento de la empresa*. Harvard Business ReviewBilbao: Deusto.

Duronio, Margaret, and Bruce Loessin. 1993. 9 – Management effectiveness in Fundraising. *Governing, Leading, and Managing Nonprofit Organizations – New Insights From Research and Practice*. 170–90. San Francisco: Jossey-Bass Publishers.

Edwards, Michael, and David Hulme. 1996. *Non-governmental Organisations. Performance and Accountability. Beyond the Magic Bullet*. London: Earthscan. Publications Ltd.

Embley, Lawrence. 1993. 9 – Initiating a Philanthropic Business Strategy. *Doing Well While Doing Good – The Marketing Lonk between Business & Nonprofit Causes*. Lawrencew Embley, 217–44. New Jersey: Prentice Hall.

Esteller, Xavier. 2001. Aproximació als Consells d'Administració de les Organitzacions No Lucratives. *Tesina De Licenciatura - ESADE Barcelona*.

European Commission 2001. *Green Paper – Promoting a European Framework for Corporate Social Responsibility*. Brussels: European Union.

Evers, Adalbert, and Ivan Svetlik eds. 1993. *Balancing Pluralism. New Welfare Mixes in Care for the Elderly*. Aldershot, England: Ashgate Publishing Company.

Evers, Adalbert, and Helmut Wintersberger. 1990. *Shifts in the Welfare Mix: Their Impact on Work, Social Services, and Welfare Policies*. Vienna: European Centre for Social Welfare Policy and Research.

Ferris, J., and E. Graddy. 1986. Contracting Out: For What? With Whom? *Public Administration Review*, 46, no. 4: 332–44.

Firstenberg, Paul. (1996). 10 – A Marketing Approach to Fundraising. *The 21st Century Nonprofit – Remaking the Organization in the Post-government Era*. Paul Firstenberg: The Foundation Center, 117–53.

Fundació Catalana de l'Esplai. 2000. *Memoria de actividades 1996–1999*. Barcelona: Fundació Catalana de l'Esplai.

Gardner, John W. 1990. *On Leadership*. New York: Free Press.

Giddens, Anthony. 2000. *The Third Way and Its Critics*. Cambridge: Polity Press.

Gilbert, Neil. 1985. The Commercialization of Social Welfare. *The Journal of Applied Behavioral Science*, 21, no. 4: 365–76.

Goldberg, Peter. 1990. 21 – Corporate Social Responsibility and Public-private Partnerships. *The Future of the Nonprofit Sector – Challenges, Changes and Policy Considerations*, ed. Virginia Hodgkinson, and Richard Lyman, 341–52. San Francisco and London: Jossey-Bass Publications.

Gray, John. 2000. *Two Faces of Liberalism*. Polity Press.

———. 2001. *Las dos caras del liberalismo*. Barcelona: Paidos.

Greiner, L. 1972. *Evolution and Revolution as Organizations Grow, Harvard Business Review*. July–August.

Greiner, L. E. 1967. Antecedents of Planned Organization Change. *The Journal of Applied Behavioral Science* 3: 51–85.

Hatch, S., and I. Mocroft. 1983. *Components of Welfare*. London: Bedford Square Press.

Hatry, H., van Houten, T., Plantz, M. C., and Greenway, M. T. 1996. *Measuring Program Outcomes: A Practical Approach*. Alexandria, VA: United Way of America.

Heap, Simon. 2000. NGO-business Partnerships: Research-in-Progress. *Public Management (UK)* 2, no. 4.

Henry Hansmann. 1987. Economic Theories of Nonprofit Organization, in The Nonprofit Sector: A Research Handbook, ed. Walter W. Powell. New Haven: Yale University Press.

Herzlinger, Regina E. 1996. Can Public Trust in Nonprofits and Governments Be Restored? *Harvard Business Review*, 74(2): 97–107

Himmelstein, Jerome. 1997. 2 – The Making of Corporate Philanthropy. *Looking Good and Doing Good – Corporate Philanthropy and Corporate Power*. Jerome Himmelstein, 14–74. Indiana University Press.

Hirschman, A. O. 1970. *Exit, Voice and Loyalty. Responses to Decline, in Firms, Organization and States*, edn. Cambridge, Ma: Harvard University Press.

Hirschman, Albert. 1992. *Rivals Views of Market Society and Other Recent Essays*. Cambridge, MA: Harvard University Press.

Hodgkinson, Virginia A., and Murray Weitzman. 1994. *Giving and Volunteering in the United States*. Washington, DC: Independent Sector.

Hood, C., and Schuppert, G. F. 1988. *Delivering Public Services in Western Europe*. London: Sage.

Huxham, Chris. 1996. *Creating Collaborative Advantage*. London: SAGE.

Independent Sector 2001. *Giving and Volunteering in the United States*. Washington: Independent Sector.

Itriago, M. A., and A. Itriago. 2000. *Las redes: el cambio social*. Caracas: Sinergia.

James, Estelle. 1983. How Nonprofits Grow: A Model. *Journal of Policy Analysis and Management* 2: 350–66.

Jeavons, Thomas H. 2001. Ethics in Nonprofit Management. Creating a Culture of Integrity. *Understanding Nonprofits Organizations. Governance, Leadership and Management*, ed. Steven J. OttBoulder: Westview Press.

Kearns, Kevin P. 1996. *Managing for Accountability*. San Francisco: Jossey-Bass.

Kettner, Peter M., and Lawrence L. Martin. 1987. *Purchase of Service Contracting*. Newbury Park, CA: SAGE Publications, Inc.

Klemp, G. O. 1980. *The Assessment of Occupational Competency*. Report to the National Institute of Education, Washington DC, USA.

Kolderie, Ted. 1986. The Two Different Concepts of Privatization. *Public Administration Review* 46, no. 4: 285–91.

Kramer, Ralph. 1981. *Voluntary Agencies in the Welfare State*. Berkeley and Los Angeles, CA: University of California Press.

———. 1985. The Future of the Voluntary Agency in a Mixed Economy. *The Journal of Applied Behavioral Science* 21, no. 4: 377–91.

Kramer, Ralph, and Bart Grossman. 1987. Contracting for Social Services: Process Management and Resource Dependencies. *Social Service Review* 61: 32–55.

Kumar, Sarabajava. 1997. *Accountability in the Contract State: The Relationships Between Voluntary Organisations, Local Government and Service Users*. York: The Joseph Rowntree Foundation.

Le Grand, Julian. 1991. Quasi-markets and social policy. *Economic Journal* 101: 1256–67.

———. 1992. *Paying or providing for welfare?, Studies in Decentralisation and Quasi-Markets no 15*. Bristol: SAUS, University of Bristol.

Le Monde. 1998. EMPLOI. un peu plus d'une embauche sur cinq s'est faite en contrat à durée indéterminée en. February 3rd, Paris.

Leat, Diana. 1996. Are Voluntary Organisations Accountable? *Voluntary Agencies. Challenges of Organization and Management*. David Billis, and Margaret Harris. London: Macmillan Press.

Light, Paul C. 2002. *Pathways to Nonprofit Excellence*. Washington, DC: Brookings Institution.

Light. 2004. *Sustaining Nonprofit Performance: The Case for Capacity Building and the Evidence to Support It*. Brookings Institution, 2004.

Lindenberg, Marc, and J. Patrick Dobel. 1999. The Challenges of Globalization for Northern International Relief and Development NGO. *Nonprofit and Voluntary Sector Quarterly* 28, no. 4.

Lindenberg, Marc, and Coralie Bryant. 2001. Going Global. Transforming Relief and Development NGO. West Hartford: Kumarian Press.

Longo, Francisco. 2004. *Mérito y flexibilidad. La gestión de las personas en las organizaciones del sector público*. Barcelona: Paidós Empresa.

Lozano, Josep M. 2001. L'empresa en la societat. *IDEES*, no. 10.

Macneil, Ian R. 1974. The Many Futures of Contracts. *Southern California Law Review* 47: 691–816.

Madrid, Antonio. 1997. El derecho en las organizaciones no gubernamentales. En *¿Trabajo voluntario o participación?* Ariel Jerez (coordinador). Madrid: Editorial Tecnos.

Maru File, Karen, and Russ Alan Prince. 1995. Cause-related Marketing, Philanthropy, and the Arts. *Nonprofit Management & Leadership* 5, no. 3: 249–60.

McCarthy, Kathleen, Hodgkinson, Virginia, Sumariwalla, Russy *et al.* 1992. *The Nonprofit Sector in the Global Community: Voices from Many Nations.* San Francisco: Jossey-Bass Publishers.

McKinsey and Company. 2001. *Effective Capacity Building in Nonprofit Organizations.* Venture Philanthropy Partners.

Melendez, Sarah. 2001. Colaboracion entre ONL y empresas.

Mendoza, Xavier. 1990. Técnicas gerenciales y modernización de la administración pública en España. *Documentación Administrativa,* no. 223: 261–90.

———. 1991. *Algunas reflexiones acerca de la "transición al mercado" de los servicios sociales.* Barcelona: Jornadas Público-Privado y Bienestar Social.

———. 1995. *Las transformaciones del sector público en las democracias avanzadas: del Estado del bienestar al Estado relacional,* edn. Santander: Universidad Internacional Menéndez y Pelayo.

Minow, Martha. 2002. Partners not Rivals. Boston: Beacon Press.

Miralles, Josep. 2002. Responsabilitat Empresarial. *XII Congrés de Valors d'Empresa i Societat.*

Morley, Elaine, Elisa Vinson, and Harry P. Hatry. 2001. *Outcome Measurement in Nonprofit Organizations: Current Practices and Recommendations.* Washington: Independent Sector and The Urban Institute.

Morris, Burnis. 1998. *A Journalist's Guide. Covering Nonprofit Organizations and Their People.* Washington: Independent Sector.

Murray, V., and Tassie, R. 1994. *Evaluating the Effectiveness of Nonprofit Organizations,* ed. Robert D. Herman. The Jossey-Bass Handbook of Nonprofit Leadership and Management (pp. 303–24). San Francisco: Jossey-Bass.

Osborne, David, and Ted Gaebler. 1993. *Reinventing Government.* New York, NY: Plume.

Ospina, Sonia, Bethany Godsoe, and Ellen Schall. 2002. Co-producing Knowledge: Practitioners and Scholars Working Together to Understand Leadership. Leadership for a Changing World.

Oster, Sharon. 1995. 8 – Fundraising for Nonprofits. *Strategic Management for Nonprofit Organisations – Theory and Cases.* Sharon Oster, 107–21. New York and London: Oxford University Press.

Peter F. Drucker. 1996. *The Executive in Action.* New York, NY: HarperBusiness.

Peter Senge. 1990. *The Fifth Discipline: The Art and Practice of the Learning Organization.* New York: Doubleday.

Plataforma de ONGs de Acción Social. 2003. *Como trabajar mejor juntos.* Madrid: Plataforma de ONGs de Acción Social.

Prats i Cátala, Joan. 2000. *Reiventar la Burocracia y construir la nueva gerencia pública.* En Pensar lo Público, coordinado por Francisco Longo y Manuel Zafra. Granada, Unión Iberoamericana de Municipalistas, 2000.

Putnam, Robert D. 2000. *Bowling Alone.* New York, NY: Simon & Schuster.

Rojas Marcos, Luis. 2001. El voluntariado es bueno para la salud. *El Pais* : 16.

Rough, Jim. 1998. *We're Still Learning How to Count! Lessons Learned from the Annual Project Information, 1997.* CARE.

Rugman, Alan M. 2001. Mastering Management 13 – The Illusion of the Global Company. *Financial Times* January, no. 8.

Ruyra de Andrade, Margarita, and Ignacio Sotelo-Zuloaga Galdiz. 1999. Patrocinio de las grandes compañias españolas: informacion al accionista y legitimidad de las actuaciones. *ICI Tribuna Economica,* no. 777: 125–38.

Sagawa, Shirley, and Eli Segal. 1999. Common Interest, Common Good. *HBS Working Knowledge.*

Salamon, Lester. 1981. Rethinking Public Management: Third-Party Government and the Changing Forms of Government Action. *Public Policy* 29, no. 3: 255–75.

——. 1987. Partners in Public Service: The Scope and Theory of Government-Nonprofit Relations. *The Nonprofit Sector: A Research Handbook.* Walter Powell. New Haven, CT: Yale University Press.

Salamon, Lester. 1995. *Partners in Public Service: Government–Nonprofit Relations in the Modern Welfare State.* Baltimore, Maryland: Johns Hopkins University Press.

Salamon, L. M., and H. K. Anheier. 1997. *The Challenge of Definition: Thirteen Realities in Search of a Concept. Defining the Nonprofit Sector: A Cross-National Analysis.* Manchester, Manchester University Press.

Salamon, Lester M., and Anheier, Helmut K. 1998. Social Origins of Civil Society: Explaining the Nonprofit Sector Cross-Nationally. *Voluntas: International Journal of Voluntary and Nonprofit Organizations.* 9, 3, 213–248.

Sargeant, Adrian, and Juergen Kaehler. 1998. *Benchmarking Charity Costs. Research Report 5.* Kent: Charities Aid Foundation.

Savas, Emanuel. 1987. *Privatization. The Key to Better Government.* Chatham, NJ: Chatham House Publishers.

Saxon-Harrold, S., and A. Hefron. 2001. *Research Giving. Facts and Findings, Crossing the Border, Competition and Collaboration Among Nonprofits, Business and Governments.* Washington DC: Independent sector.

Schmidheiny, Stephan. 1992. *Cambiando el rumbo. Una perspectiva global del empresariado para el desarrollo y el medio ambiente.* México: Fondo de Cultura Económica.

Schuppert, G. F., and C. Hood. 1998. *Delivering Public Services in Western Europe. Sharing Western European Experiences of Para-governmental Organisation.* London: Sage.

Sciullo, Jean di. 1993. 7 – El mecenatge d'emopresara aplicat a causes socials i humanitaries. *Marketing i comunicacio de les institucions.* Jean di Sciullo, 348–68. Edicions Pleniluni.

Smith, Hayden. 1989. 20 – Corporate Contributions to the Year 2000: Growth or Decline? *The Future of the Nonprofit Sector – Challenges, Changes and Policy Considerations.* Virginia Hodgkinson, and Richard Lyman, 315–40. San Francisco and London: Jossey-Bass Publications.

Smith, Steven, and Michael Lipsky. 1993. *Nonprofits for Hire. The Welfare State in the Age of Contracting.* Cambridge, Massachusetts: Harvard University Press.

Taylor, Marilyn. 1990. *New Times, New Challenges: Voluntary Organisations Facing 1990.* London, UK: National Council for Voluntary Organisations.

——. 1992. The Changing Role of the Nonprofit Sector in Britain: Moving Toward the Market. *Government and the Thrid Sector,* eds, Benjamin Gidron, Ralph M. Kramer, and Lester M. SalamonSan Francisco, CA: Jossey-Bass.

The Aspen Institute 2001. *Competing Visions: The Nonprofit Sector in The Twenty-First Century.* Aspen (Co.): The Aspen Institute.

Tschirhart, Mary. 1996. *Artful Leadership.* Bloomington: Indiana University Press.

Turull and Negre, J. 2002. Les relacions interassociatives: El treball en xarxa. *Congrés De Les Associacions.*

Ullman, C. F. 1998. *The Welfare State Other Crisis: Explaining the New Partnership Between Nonprofit Organisations and the State in France.* Bloomington: Indiana University Press.

Useem, Michael. 1987. Corporate Philanthropy. *The Nonprofit Sector – A Research Handbook.* Walter Powell, 340–59. New Haven and London: Yale University Press.

Valente, Carl, and Lydia Manchester. 1984. *Rethinking Local Services: Examining Alternative Delivery Approaches.* Washington, DC: ICMA.

Vernis, Alfred. 1994. La gestión de las organizaciones no lucrativas. *Papers ESADE*.

——. 1998a. Los retos en la gestión de las organizaciones no lucrativas. *Revis ta L' Associació de Barcelona L'Associació*. Novembre-Desembre.

——. 1998b. *La mejora de la gestión y la creación de empleo en las organizaciones no lucrativas*. Barcelona Management Review, Vol. 8. Mayo-Agosto.

——. 1999a. *El reto de explicar a la sociedad las realizaciones de las organizaciones no lucrativas*. Barcelona: Torre Jussana-Ayuntamiento de Barcelona.

——. 1999b. La necessitat urgent de guanyar ara la confiança de la societat. *Revista L'Associació de Barcelona*. Gener-Febrer.

——. 2000a. Organizing Services to the Elderly: A Tale of Two Cities. Tesis doctoral. New York: New York University.

——. 2000b. La relación público-privado en la provisión de servicios sociales. Capítulo en *Pensar lo Público*, coordinado por Francisco Longo y Manuel Zafra. Granada, Unión Iberoamericana de Municipalistas.

——. 2001a. Ganar legitimidad mejorando la gestión. *La Vanguardia* marzo.

——. 2001b. *Los diferentes elementos de la rendición de cuentas en las organizaciones no lucrativas*. Madrid: Fundación Lealtad y Comunidad Autónoma de Madrid.

——. 2003a. Reflexiones a raíz del estudio del tercer sector en España. En Victor Pérez Díaz: *El tercer sector social en España*. Madrid: Ministerio de Trabajo y Asuntos Sociales.

——. 2003b. Administracions públiques i organitzacions no lucratives a Catalunya: de la relació a la col·laboració. En el libro *Llibre Blanc del Tercer Sector Civicsocial*. Barcelona: Centre d'Estudis de Temes Contemporanis.

——. 2003c. El balance social y la rendición de cuentas del tercer sector. Capítulo 35 del libro: *La economía social y el tercer sector. España y el entorno europeo*. Madrid: Escuela Libre Editorial.

——. 2003d. La relación de las Fundaciones con los patronatos. En *Estudi de les Fundacions Catalanes*. Barcelona: Coordinadora Catalana de Fundaciones.

Vernis, Alfred, Maria Iglesias, Beatriz Sanz, Maria Solernou, Jaume Urgell, and Pau Vidal. 1998. *La gestión de las organizaciones no lucrativas*. Barcelona: Ed.Deusto.

Weisbrod, Burton A. 1988. *The Nonprofit Economy*. Cambridge, MA: Harvard University Press.

William G. Bowen. 1994. *Inside the Boardroom: Governance by Directors and Trustees*, (San Francisco, CA: Jossey-Bass.

Wolch, Jennifer. 1990. *The Shadow State: Government and Voluntary Sector in Transition*. New York: The Foundation Center.

Yankey, John. 1996. 2 – Corporate Support of Nonprofit Organizations – Partnerships Across the Sectors. *Corporate Philanthropy at the Crossroads*. Dwight Burlingame, and Dennis Young, 7–22. Indiana University Press.

Index